Cannibalism

the text of this book is printed on 100% recycled paper

Human Aggression

CANNIBALISM

and Cultural Form

ELI SAGAN

Foreword by
Robert N. Bellah

HARPER TORCHBOOKS
Harper & Row, Publishers
New York, Evanston, San Francisco, London

CANNIBALISM: HUMAN AGGRESSION AND CULTURAL FORM

LIBRARY OF CONGRESS CATALOG CARD NUMBER: 74–2073
First HARPER TORCHBOOK edition published 1974.

A hardcover edition of this book is published by Harper & Row.

STANDARD BOOK NUMBER: 06–131830–2 (PAPERBACK)
STANDARD BOOK NUMBER: 06–136154–2 (HARDCOVER)

Deeply troubled, Zeus who gathers the clouds answered her:

"Dear lady, what can be all the great evils
  done to you
by Priam and the sons of Priam, that you
  are thus furious
forever to bring down the strong-founded
  city of Ilion?
If you could walk through the gates and
  through the towering ramparts
and eat Priam and the children of Priam
  raw, and the other
Trojans, then, then only might you glut at
  last your anger.
Do as you please then." . . .

—Homer *Iliad*

CONTENTS

Foreword ix
Preface xiii
Introduction xv
1. Aggressive Cannibalism 1
2. Affectionate Cannibalism 22
3. The Sublimation of Aggressive Cannibalism: Head-Hunting 35
4. Sacrifice: The Formal Reconciliation of Aggression and Affection 48
5. The Psychological Origin of Aggression 64
6. The Uses of Aggression 83
7. Religion and Aggression: The Sacred and the Secular 99
8. Sublimation 111
9. The Ambiguity of Development 132
Index 145

FOREWORD

This book represents a combination of disciplined research, theoretical clarity, and moral imagination that is rare in American intellectual life. Mr. Sagan has taken cannibalism—at first sight a most unpromising, indeed repulsive subject—as a point of departure for careful theorizing and daring speculation on the roles of aggression and love in human life. It is the choice of subject that is in the first instance so striking. Cannibalism is widely reported in the anthropological literature, frequent in myths in many cultures and in fairy tales in our own culture, and occasionally front-page news, as in the 1972 airplane crash in the mountains of Chile. Yet, aside from considerable psychoanalytic work on cannibalistic fantasies, little has been written to illuminate the cultural and historical meaning of this practice. The many monographs describing actual cases have not been used in this instance as in so many others for the construction of general theory, though that use, as Clyde Kluckhohn said long ago, is the chief justification for undertaking field research in the first place. Mr. Sagan suggests that the taboo on cannibalism has become transformed into a taboo on thinking about cannibalism; we should be grateful to him for breaking that taboo.

There are several respects in which this is a notable study even beyond its contribution to our understanding of cannibalism and its prohibition in human history. The chief theoretical resource for the study is drawn from Sigmund Freud, although it is a cultural and historical study and not a study of an individual biography. It thus falls under the rubric of psychohistory or psychoanalytic sociology. But unlike the authors of many studies in this genre, Mr. Sagan has a grasp on the nature of socio-cultural process that prevents him from reducing it to direct psychological expression. Indeed, socio-cultural process is itself seen as actively contributing to change in personality structure throughout history. It is precisely the mediating process between culture and personality in which Mr. Sagan is interested—he does not seek to reduce one level to the other. His use of the concepts of symbolic form and sublimation contribute significantly to our understanding of this process of mediation. Because of the seriousness with which he takes the possibility that cultural form can transmute even very deep psychological motives, his contribution to the psychoanalytic concept of sublimation is a significant one (see especially chapter 8). It is in his discussion of cultural form and its capacity to transform motivation that Mr. Sagan makes notable contributions to the understanding of ritual and religion, particularly in evolutionary perspective.

The uncompromising evolutionary stance of this book is another of its significant features. In recent years, social evolution has again become respectable in anthropology and sociology, but the commonest form is that based primarily on economic or technological determinism. Mr. Sagan, however, joins the minority of social evolutionists who consider the evolution of symbolic form—religion and morality—a major dimension of evolutionary change at least partly independent of economics and technology. My only quarrel with Mr. Sagan's presentation is his definition of religion in terms of classical theism, which is serviceable enough for his purposes but too narrow in my opinion to deal with advanced historic and modern religions. Thus, I would interpret the notion of the sublimation of religion into art as presented in chapter 8 as a transformation of one kind of religion into another. But the essential point is that the forms of religion change in an orderly evolutionary way, as indicated by the fact from which the book starts: once cannibalism was widespread and religiously sanctioned; now it is everywhere religiously taboo.

Finally, I would like to underline the fact that this book is an expression not only of disciplined scholarship but of moral imagination. The moral concern of the book, far from limiting its value as scholarship, has operated continually to broaden and deepen the intellectual problems with which it deals. Moral concern, frankly acknowledged, allows the reader to judge whether or not the writer's biases have influenced his interpretation of the data. Mr. Sagan is not "value neutral" any more than Max Weber was. He tries not to let his value commitments dictate his findings, but it is his moral passion that gives his work its intellectual seriousness. "Mind in the service of eros" might be a valid motto for Freud's lifework. In that respect, Mr. Sagan is a worthy disciple.

ROBERT N. BELLAH

PREFACE

If one is fortunate, one has certain people to thank—people who have given the kind of help that makes a book significantly better than it would have been without their aid. Such good fortune has been mine. I am deeply indebted to the following people, and it is a pleasure for me to acknowledge their help.

Donald Cutler has edited and guided the manuscript from its first draft. He has given time and energy to it beyond any obligation. Working with him has been a great personal pleasure.

Lee Halprin read every draft of the work with scrupulous care. His advice has been invaluable in clearing up points of style and, more important, in demanding consistency and clarity of intellectual expression; he has been for me the best kind of critic.

Robert Bellah has encouraged me, for many years, in my intellectual efforts, consistently urging me to write down my ideas.

This book is dedicated to my wife, Frimi. It may seem strange, at first, to so dedicate a book about human aggression. The reader will find, however, that this work is as much about eros, in all its manifold meanings, as it is about destructiveness. The dedication, therefore, becomes not only natural but appropriate to the work itself.

I am grateful to the following publishers for granting me permission to quote extracts from their books: The Macmillan Company for *Our Primitive Contemporaries* by George P. Murdock; the Canadian publishers McClelland and Stewart Limited, and the University of Washington Press for *Indians of the North Pacific Coast* by Tom McFeat, a volume of the Carleton Library Series; and W. W. Norton for *Civilization and Its Discontents* by Sigmund Freud, edited and translated by James Strachey.

INTRODUCTION

With pitifully few exceptions, almost all human societies have exercised some form of institutionalized aggression, directing it inward against a group of people within the society or outward against another society; some cultures have sought both modes of aggressive satisfaction. This aggression has not been of an individual or illegal nature—it has not been the behavior of a small number of aberrant people performing asocial acts. We are concerned here with that form of social aggression that societies have certified as legitimate and moral. When a society commits an act of social aggression—such as the enslavement of a group of human beings—this slavery has the sanction of the whole community. It is society *as society* expressing aggression that is the subject of this book.

Kant has asserted that the basic ground of immorality is the viewing of other people as objects. We may define human social aggression as the systematic, recurrent, legitimatized treatment as objects of one group of people by another.

All societies that have practiced social aggression have done so by asserting, implicitly or explicitly, that certain groups of human beings are not human and are, therefore, legitimate objects of aggression. Such societies divide the human world into those who are human (we) and those who are subhuman (them). The list of "them" is a catalogue of the oppressed, dominated, and exploited peoples of the history of the world: black people in a white society, infidels for the Turks, heretics for the Christians, barbarians for the Romans, slaves of all kinds, unorganized workers in a capitalist society, intellectuals in Soviet Russia, non-European peoples in the age of imperialism, German Jews, the subject states of Assyria, the sacrificed captive for the Aztec, the dead prisoner for the head-hunter, women for most men, and the cannibal victim for the cannibal.

Institutionalized social aggression must be analyzed and understood separately from individual, personal aggression. Social aggression has its origins in psychological aggression, but the process of institutionalizing an individual psychological attitude is very complex. That process consists, in part, of the creation and implementation of cultural form, and such form is not capable of being reduced to a psychological phenomenon. It was said in ancient Rome that all senators were good people, but the Senate was a wild beast. The goal of this book is to try to understand why it is that "good" people create institutions that act like wild beasts—why it is that human history has provided us with such a long list of those who have been the unhappy objects of human aggression.

This tragic tale, however, is only half the story. Throughout history, human beings demonstrate an equally extraordinary capacity to renounce aggression and to widen the definition of *human* to include more and more of the people in the world. Christianity puts an end to the barbarism of the Roman arena and proclaims that even a slave has a soul, Islam puts an end to female infanticide, slavery practically disappears from the world, the barbarisms of early industrial capitalism are renounced, democracy asserts the individual worth of all in society, the noncannibal head-hunter renounces the great aggressive pleasure of eating human flesh.

We live, in fact, on the verge of a great moral revolution. For the first time in the history of the world, a large number of people—not just a few moral geniuses—are willing to assert that the idea of *human* is to be extended to all human beings, that no one is to be excluded from the human definition. This has never been true before. Whether such a humane attitude will become the predominant form of various world cultures remains to be seen.

The existence of such a possibility indicates that there is a profound capacity within people to deal with, to sublimate, to renounce aggression. We are not, and have not been, helpless in the face of the pervasive power of aggression. We have created an instrument that makes it possible not to be completely overwhelmed by the destructive drives that exist in all people. Cultural form is such an instrument; the development of culture has made it possible for people to become fully human.

In our intellectual life today, there is an attitude born of the fear that if we admit that aggression is universal, or possibly even instinctual, this admission must inevitably lead to social Darwinism and fascism. Some humane, liberal-thinking people feel compelled to deny the universal existence of human aggression in order to assert that we can control our fate by the creation of a more moral culture. Culture is all, they say; there are no human instincts.

Such a point of view, while seeking to extol the power of culture, is really underestimating that power. If culture is all, its task is simple. The truth is that its task has been profoundly difficult. To say that culture has had to deal with impulses in the psyche that are in direct opposition to it does not belittle its power. It is a greater praise of culture, and much nearer the truth, to say that it has succeeded in dealing with—has succeeded in taking the power from—those universal human drives that are destructive of others and are destructive of culture itself.

Whether aggression is instinctual in all people is really not the essential question one asks in trying to understand the nature of social life. It cannot be denied that this problem is of enormous importance. For cultural form, however, the real question is not whether aggression is instinctual but whether it is *inevitable.* If it is inevitable, cultural form must deal with it no matter from where it comes. The problem "from where" is important, but it is a different problem from how culture responds to inevitable aggression.

To raise a child to become a mature, healthy, humane adult, it is not necessary to know whether psychological aggression is instinctual or not. It is, however, crucial to know whether such aggression is inevitable. The parent who attempts to forestall any manifestations of aggression in a growing child must fail in that attempt no matter how much love the child is given. The child will express aggression either because of instinct (something transmitted through the genes) or because it is impossible to live in this world without frustration, and aggression seems to be the universal human response to thwarted desire. The fact that aggression from the child is inevitable does not mean that all children grow up to be war lords, slave owners, or criminals. The manner in which the parents respond to this inevitable aggression determines, in part, what kind of adult the child becomes.

The analogy with society is precise. The fact that social aggression is inevitable does not mean that all societies are condemned to be replicas of Nazi Germany. Free democratic societies also exist, but a careful analysis of these societies would show that social aggression is expressed in them. The manner in which cultural form responds to aggression is crucial. We may hypothesize, we may work for a complex developed culture that exists without significant institutionalized aggression, but we cannot accurately claim to have seen such a society.

After many years of diligent research into the nature of culture, it would seem that the burden of proof lies not with those who advance the idea that human aggression is innate but rather with those who claim that culture is all and that there are no universal aggressive drives. A poor handful of cultures are held up as proof that people have lived without expressing any social aggression—the Pygmies and the Zuñi among them. A careful study of these cultures might reveal that they are not as unaggressive as has been asserted. Granting that certain cultural forms have been unaggressive, if culture is all and instinct nonexistent, how do we explain the fact that 99 percent of all cultures have practiced some form of institutionalized aggression? The comparative study of culture has revealed a large variation in cultural forms; the possibilities seem to be almost limitless as regards marital arrangements, sexual mores, economic systems, religious forms, comparative emphases on art, political systems, and world views. Why is it that in regard to aggression there exists almost total unanimity? If culture is free to take any path it chooses, why has it chosen this path with so much consistency?

In the pages that follow, both aspects of the question of human aggression and cultural form—the seemingly universal aggressive drive and the capacity of culture to deal with it—will be examined at length. This will be done first by looking at what appears to be the most elementary form of social aggression—cannibalism. Second, whatever valid conclusions can be drawn from this study will be applied to all cultural forms. It is the aim of this book to find certain truths about human aggression and culture that are true for all societies.

A great gulf seems to separate us from the act of cannibalism—a gulf full of horror and intense curiosity; the subject itself seems to be taboo. There must be a hundred thousand books in the English language about primitive cultures; I know of only one with cannibalism as its subject. Throughout the years of study of preliterate peoples, many aspects of their cultures have been praised as superior to our own. Certain virtues of primitive cultures have been urged upon us for emulation: some are more gentle than ours, some are sexually freer, primitive society is more cohesive, and *rites de passage* provide the growing child with a more satisfactory passage into adult life than the one of intense strain that is characteristic of adolescence in our society. Practically every aspect of primitive life has been seen by someone as superior to what we have today. No one, however, has suggested that humanity has lost touch with a basic ground of being by giving up cannibalism, and no one has urged us to readopt the practice. That far no one has seen fit to go—an indication that there is something unique about the cannibal act and our response to it.

This self-imposed taboo may be related to the intense desire to protect our conscious lives from the knowledge that we have deep, powerful aggressive feelings within ourselves. We have, however, out of an unconscious wisdom, decided not to shield our children from such feelings. Two of the most popular fairy tales of the world—*Little Red Riding Hood* and *Hansel and Gretel*—are stories about the eating or the intended eating of people; many other fairy tales deal with the same subject. Proportionately, there is more cannibalism in the stories we read our children than in the books of the anthropologists.

It is time for adults to break that taboo. It is time that we look at the most degrading thing that one human being can do to another, even if we risk finding feelings in ourselves that we wish were not there. Dostoevski wrote novels about child rapists and murderers, not in the interest of urging us to try those acts and not out of some obscene curiosity, but in the attempt to force us to see that within ourselves there lives, somewhere, such a rapist and such a murderer. The use of the imagination for this insight is an act of liberation.

It is difficult to look at the act of cannibalism, just as it is difficult to read the accounts of the concentration camps. In order to understand others, and ourselves, it is necessary to do both. "Euripides recognized, but hated Dionysus. He recognized his power, and saw that there was only one weapon to employ against him, which was to understand him and to propagate an understanding of him."[1] Human aggression, like Dionysus in Euripides' *Bacchae*, will not go away because we deny its existence. Only if we are willing to look at this destructiveness—undisguised—will we succeed in understanding and conquering it.

The first four chapters of this book are devoted to an examination of the data available from cannibal societies.

1. R. P. Winnington-Ingram, *Euripides and Dionysus* (Cambridge: At the University Press, 1948), p. 179.

The fifth and sixth chapters deal with the psychological origins and uses of aggression. The last three chapters use the material discussed earlier in order to formulate theories about the nature of religion, social aggression, and cultural form.

Cannibalism

Aggressive

1

Cannibalism

There have been occasions when people under circumstances of extreme stress resorted to cannibalism to assuage hunger that could not be satisfied in any other way. Instances of shipwreck and siege provided such occasions. During the siege of Leningrad in World War II, not only did people cut the flesh from dead corpses and use it for food, but the more criminal elements of society deliberately murdered human beings, eating the flesh for their own sustenance and selling whatever was left over.[1] But this study is not concerned with cannibalism in unusual and desperate circumstances as a final act of survival.

Our interest is in those societies that practice cannibalism on a regular basis, as an accepted mode of behavior regulated by rules that indicate when, where, and how it should be practiced. In some societies, *anthropophagy* (*anthropo*, "man"; *phagous*, "eating") is institutionalized; the society dictates to its members the manner and methods of eating other people.

Institutionalized cannibalism is found only in those societies that we call "primitive"—simple, preliterate cultures that are studied by anthropologists—as distinguished from complex, literate cultures that are studied by sociologists. The Aztecs developed a literate, complex culture, and, yet, they

1. Harrison E. Salisbury, *The 900 Days* (New York: Harper & Row, 1969), pp. 479–481.

practiced cannibalism to a very limited degree. But they are the only known exception to the rule that cannibalism is practiced only by primitive societies. No evidence of cannibalism appears in the early histories of Egypt, Mesopotamia, or the Aegean.

The word *cannibalism* describes the act of one human being eating a part or the whole body of another human being. In some instances, only the blood is drunk, and no part of the body is eaten; in other cases, only a part of the victim is eaten, so that it is possible that the victim remains alive. Some tribes kill people for the express purpose of eating them; others eat only those who have died of natural or accidental causes. All of these various situations are designated *cannibalism* even though the psychological and social implications of these various activities may differ greatly.

There is no survey in existence that indicates what proportion of primitive societies have practiced cannibalism. From the available information, it appears that a great many have and a great many have not. Certainly, more societies have not practiced it; yet equally certainly, it has not been a rare occurrence. George Murdock in *Our Primitive Contemporaries*[2] presents a general survey of eighteen primitive societies. Five of these definitely have engaged in some sort of cannibal behavior; in two more, cannibalism is possible but not definitely established. The incidence of cannibalism described in Murdock's study is consistent with a general impression one gets from reading broadly in ethnographic literature.

Cannibalism has been practiced in all parts of the world. There is evidence of it among North American Indians, South American Indians, tribes in Africa and Australia, and all through the Pacific. The most interesting data, however, comes from a few places—Fiji, New Guinea, northwest America, Nigeria, the Congo, and Australia. It is not necessarily true that these areas held a concentration of cannibalistic societies. In part, our knowledge of cannibalism

2. George P. Murdock, *Our Primitive Contemporaries* (New York: Macmillan, 1934).

results from the fact that anthropologists studied these areas while cannibalism was still flourishing. Under the impact of European imperialism, cannibalism has been gradually abandoned in almost all societies.

Some cannibal victims are members of the tribes that eat them; others are outsiders. This is a crucial distinction. When members of the same tribe are eaten, these people—with very rare exceptions—have not been killed in order to be eaten. They have died an ordinary death, and the eating of parts of their bodies is an integral part of the funeral customs of the tribe. It does happen on occaison that a member of the tribe is killed and his body eaten, but such activity is exceptional, as we shall observe later on. Most human beings who are killed in order that they may be eaten are not members of the tribe doing the eating. In these cases (that is, the eating of outsiders), which include the largest number of instances of cannibalism, the killing is as central a motive as the eating.

For the cannibal who eats people outside his tribe, warfare and cannibalism are inexorably connected. It is as natural for him to eat the bodies of those he has slain as it was for the Viking to plunder the cities of northern France that he destroyed. With the Viking, it was impossible to say what was the prime motive in his behavior—the killing or the plundering. Similarly, one cannot say of the cannibal that he makes war in order to obtain bodies to eat or that making war and killing others are his prime motives and the eating of his victims merely an incidental pleasure. His desire is to make war, kill people, and eat them.

In New Guinea, the Tugarians were a savage, warlike, and cruel tribe who tyrannized villages along the coast west of the Baxter River. Like their Viking counterparts, these pirates used long, fleet canoes, stealing along the coast and up the rivers and creeks, plundering, murdering, and taking prisoners. In order to prevent the prisoners from fighting or running away, the Tugarian warriors would break their arms and legs, keeping them alive, however, so that their supply of meat would stay fresh until it was needed. The Tugarians would spend several months on such voyages before returning home. The captured prisoners were their assurance that they would not run out of fresh provisions during the length of the voyage.[3]

In Polynesia, women and priests were enlisted so that a victory feast would be a joyous occasion.

> They pick out the good bodies of the slain for the oven, and throw the bad away; they tie up a captive to a tree, dig a hole, and kindle a hot stone-oven for his body before his very eyes. The women go to battle. They keep to the rear, and attend to the *commissariat!* Whenever they see one of the enemy fall, it is their business to rush forward, pull the body behind, and dress it for the oven. The hands are the choice bits, sacred to the priests. The priests go to battle, but sit in the distance, *fasting* and praying for victory. . . . If the body of a chief is cooked, everyone must partake, down to the little child, and before a gourmandizer proceeds to polish the bones, he calls out, "Have all tasted?" If it is the body of a woman, they eat only the arms and legs. On Mare they devour all. Sometimes they cook in joints, and sometimes the whole body is doubled up in a sitting position with the knees to the chin, put into the oven, and served up so, as they squat around for their meal. Their appetite for human flesh is never satisfied. "Do you mean to say that you will forbid us the *fish of the sea*? Why, these are our fish!" This is how they talk when you speak against cannibalism.[4]

The descriptions of the Tugarians and Polynesians are not unusual. From these examples, one learns two very important aspects of cannibalism. First, the cannibal enjoys eating human flesh: he likes the taste, he takes pleasure in the human feast, and he strongly resists efforts to make him abandon the practice. Cannibalism is not a deep, dark, repulsive ritual imposed on people by a tyrannical priesthood. The cannibal does not claim that he dislikes the experience or that he does it only to obtain benefits such as fertility of the soil or a cure for disease. The eating of human flesh is, for

3. S. McFarlane, *Among the Cannibals of New Guinea* (London, 1888), pp. 105–106.

4. G. Turner, *Nineteen Years in Polynesia* (London, 1861), pp. 426–427.

him, a positive and pleasurable act. However, the act of eating others can also be an occasion for fear and ambivalence.

Second, eating the vanquished is as important to warfare as victory is. For the cannibal, many metaphors are reduced to literalness: the fruits of victory are literally eaten. In the relation of warfare and cannibalism, we can begin to see that cannibalism is closely connected with the expression and satisfaction of human aggression. I define *aggression* as the desire to dominate or tyrannize another person or other people. Warfare, unlike private aggression, is a function of society as a whole; it is an institutionalized form of aggression. It is an attempt of one whole society to dominate or tyrannize another society. The human desire for revenge—to hurt or kill someone who has injured oneself—is one of the mainsprings of human aggression. In primitive societies, the satisfaction of private vengeance follows definite prescribed rules. In primitive and complex societies, retribution often becomes a matter for the society as a whole. In this case, the tribe seeks the satisfaction of revenge in an institutionalized context. In many primitive societies, revenge is a constant affair between tribes and is frequently the motive for warfare, killing, and anthropophagy. For a cannibal, the ultimate satisfaction of vengeance is to eat one's victim.

Remarking on the cannibals of Melanesia, Seligmann writes:

> In the vast majority of cases of cannibalism in the south-eastern district the eating of human flesh was part of the solemn act of revenge which it was the duty of each community to take on behalf of its own members killed and eaten by other communities with whom it was at enmity. . . . prisoners taken in warfare were brought alive to the hamlet-group where they would be tortured before being killed and eaten. This apparently occurred only when a prisoner was to be killed in payment for the death of a member of the captor's community, and in spite of the pleasure to be derived from a cannibal feast it was clear that commonly prisoners would only be tortured and killed in such numbers

> that their deaths made the score even between their community and that of their captors.[5]

Obviously, something would then happen to make the score uneven so that the process of capturing, torturing, and eating could begin all over again. What strikes us in these situations of revenge "to even the score" is that stability is rarely achieved and peace does not become a reality. It seems probable that the warring, torturing, and eating are desired for their own sake.

In Orokaiva, the widow of a slain warrior was compelled to stay in seclusion until a victim was secured from the tribe that had killed him; the body of this revenge victim was served up at the feast that marked the end of her seclusion.[6] On Molot, a slain man's house was left standing and kept in good repair; his spears and tomahawks were placed inside it. Nearby, a *ragan* ("dead tree") was erected with a small platform in the branches; whenever the family feasted on anything good to eat, a small portion was put on the platform for the dead man's spirit. The people of the village were constantly on the lookout for someone from the village of the killer. Sometimes, people from a third village captured prisoners from the killer's village. Emissaries from the murdered man's tribe then proceeded to this third village and purchased, in whole or part, one of these captives. After cooking the revenge victim's flesh, all the men, women, and children of the family of the first murdered man ate a small portion; another portion was put on the *ragan* as an offering to the murdered man's spirit. Then, everyone beat the bushes, shouted, and made all kinds of noise to drive the spirit away; the *ragan* was pulled up and thrown away, and the spears and tomahawks were removed from the house and left to rot. The revenge was complete; peace had been made with the dead man's spirit.[7]

5. C. G. Seligmann, *The Melanesians of British New Guinea* (Cambridge: At the University Press, 1910), pp. 548, 569–570.
6. F. E. Williams, *Orokaiva Society* (London: Oxford University Press, 1930), p. 218.
7. George Brown, *Melanesians and Polynesians* (London: Macmillan & Co., 1910), pp. 140–142.

One can imagine a noncannibalistic tribe behaving in exactly the same way, except for the act of eating the revenge victim's flesh. Sadistic and brutal revenge is not the prerogative of the cannibal alone. For him, however, all aggression must ultimately be satisfied in the mouth and in the stomach.

All societies have institutionalized models of manliness to which young boys are expected to conform if they are to grow into adult men. These forms of manliness include aggressive actions (warring, raiding, killing, hunting, fighting, competing with other men for victories) as well as beneficent activities (providing for the spiritual or physical well-being of those around one; increasing the intellectual, artistic, technological, magical, or moral knowledge of the community). There is great variation among cultures in the degree to which aggressive activities, as opposed to beneficent ones, play a part in the definition of manliness. This is true whether one is examining primitive tribes or modern societies; both may be either highly aggressive or strongly pacific. If one looks carefully at how any culture defines manly behavior, one will get a clear indication of how that culture ranks on a scale of aggressiveness. It is not surprising to find that in cannibal cultures cannibalism is an important parameter in the definition of manly behavior.

In these cultures, cannibalism is encouraged among the young, and especially among novice warriors, as an aid to becoming brave, strong, and manly. Because of the manner of education for young boys and the aggressive standard of masculine behavior, cannibal societies rank very high on any scale that measures the comparative aggressivenes of various cultures. The persistence of cannibal behavior within a primitive culture (especially when we consider that more primitive tribes were not cannibalistic than were) is a crucial indication that the culture sets a high value on aggressive behavior.

At Pulu, in the Torres Straits, tribesmen ate the heads of enemies slain in warfare. The head was cut from ear to ear and from back to front and put into an oven; the ovens were covered with stones and sand. After two bakings, the scalps came off easily without using any instruments except the hands. Small boys were forced to eat the cheeks, the eyebrows, and the balls of the eyes. Those boys who were unwilling were beaten for fear that they might become women or remain children all their lives. No man was considered fit for marriage until he had obtained such a head and presented it to his clan to eat.[8]

Also in the Torres Straits, a Mabuiag man would cut off the head of the victim and let the dripping blood fall into his mouth; he would give some of the blood to the young man who accompanied him, saying, "You do not know how to fight. You drink it and it will give you a strong heart." Tutu men drank the sweat of renowned warriors and ate scrapings from their fingernails, which had become saturated with human blood. A Tutu warrior would tear out the tongue of a man he had just killed and eat it on the spot. He would also cut off the penis of a slain enemy, preserve it, and blow through it in the direction he was going when it came time to fight again. In Nagir, in order to infuse courage into boys, a warrior would take the eye and tongue of a slain enemy, mince them, and mix them with his urine. This compound was administered to a young boy who was told to shut his eyes and not look.[9]

On Leper's Island, the eating of human flesh was believed to do its magical work even when one had not killed the victim oneself. Boys were afraid to eat the flesh but were constrained to do so because it was believed that a man-eater was afraid of nothing. Men bought flesh from someone who had killed an enemy in order that they might eat it and thereby get the name of valiant men.[10]

Anyone acquainted with primitive mentality will expect that in many cases the cannibal feels that he is absorbing the manly virtue, the courage, and the energy of the slain warrior by eating him. He is transferring to himself the *mana* ("spiritual power") of his enemy. "The women, children and un-

8. A. C. Haddon, *Head-Hunters: Black, White and Brown* (London: Methuen & Co., 1901), pp. 313–314.
9. Ibid., p. 301.
10. R. H. Codrington, *The Melanesians* (New Haven, Conn.: Hraf Press, 1957), p. 344.

initiated males were not allowed to eat human flesh. It was said to be the food of warriors only. Women and children did not need exceptional courage because they had not to go on the warpath; but their young men need it abundantly, and by eating the flesh of their victims they assume that, at the same time, they absorbed their courage and their *imunu* ("spiritual power"). Such was their stated reason for cannibalism."[11]

The same motif is repeated over and over again, specifically among the Iroquois, the Maoris, and the Solomons. *Oral incorporation* is the psychoanalytic term for such behavior. This infantile conception of reality is preserved by the cannibal throughout adult life. Young boys are taught that if they have the courage to act out such fantasies, they will become men.

Sadism, that is, human satisfaction in the suffering of others, plays a role in all cannibal activity. Some cannibal tribes engage in extremely sadistic behavior toward their victims before they are finally killed and eaten. In other tribes, the amount of overt sadistic behavior may be negligible or even nonexistent.

Even when no attempt is made to acquaint the cannibal victim with his fate, even in cases where the dead bodies of those slain in battle are eaten after the battle is over—even then there is sadistic pleasure in the eating. The cannibal's pleasure in the taste—and he tells us that the taste is excellent—is enhanced by the fact that he is eating *human* flesh—flesh that once adhered to a living human being. He cannot eat such flesh without recalling that a once-living human being is now dead, killed by someone in the cannibal's own tribe. It is reasonable to say that cannibalism is the ultimate form of sadism because it is the original form, psychologically considered. What is the worst punishment that one could inflict on someone one wished to hurt in the most radical way? Eat him, of course. The cannibal performs institutionalized acts of sadism, prescribed by the society as normal, pleasurable acts that are taught to the young as a path to adulthood.

11. J. H. Holmes, *In Primitive New Guinea* (New York: Putnam, 1924), p. 176.

In Sierra Leone, the Leopard society was a restricted, prestigious group. Many of its activities were conducted in secret. The society provided cannibal victims for its members. No attempt was made to ease the pain of the person destined to be eaten.

> The sacrificer came forward dressed in a leopard-skin, and with the leopard-knife cut open the victim's stomach from the centre towards the right side; an assistant placed a pan under the wound, and a third, inserting his hand into the wound, pulled out the liver and intestines which he placed in the pan. Now came forward five others. The first placed his hand in the wound and drew forth some fat and the four others did the same. The pan with the intestines, liver and blood was taken away to a house. The body of the victim was then carried to the piazza of the late chief's house. It being now midnight, they separated. No one was left with the victim, who was still alive and chained, and remained alive for some hours.[12]

In Fiji, one of the slaves to the king, a young girl, ran away but was soon captured and brought back to his house. At the request of the queen, the girl's arm was cut off below the elbow and cooked for the king, who ate it in her presence. The blood of Fijian people who were destined to be eaten was drunk in their presence by their torturers. Sometimes, the victim might be offered some of his own flesh to eat after his arm or his leg had been cooked. The tongues of other unfortunates would be ripped out, roasted, and eaten in front of the sufferers with taunts of "We are eating your tongues!"[13]

There are many gruesome accounts of intricate tortures prior to the eating of war capitives among the Indians of North and South America. About the Hurons it was reported:

> The captive selected as a trophy of war, to gratify their vindictive spirit, was subjected to the most inhuman and even more inquisitional torture. The nails of their fingers and toes were torn off by force; the three principle fingers used for

12. R. G. Berry, "The Sierra Leone Cannibals," *Proceedings of the Royal Irish Academy* 30 (1912): 49.

13. Garry Hogg, *Cannibalism and Human Sacrifice* (New York: Citadel, 1966), pp. 29–30.

> drawing the bow were lopped off; the skull was denuded of its hairy scalp, and coals of fire and hot ashes were heaped upon the bleeding head, or hot seething gum was poured upon it. Sometimes he was made to walk across a great number of fires with his body and feet entirely naked, between two files of tormentors who struck him with burning firebrands and rubbed his legs with heated axes. At other times they threw hot water on his back to increase his pain, and touched his fingers' ends and his sexual organs with burning cinders. Then they pierced his arm with a splint, drew out the nerves and tore them away by force. The captive remained entirely composed amidst all these agonizing tortures, singing, uttering threats against his fiendish executioners, and giving expression to his scowling hate by jeers, scoffs and words of defiance. When the victim approached the death struggle he was placed upon a scaffold; his head was cut off, his bowls were torn out, which were taken possession of by the children, who tied them to a stick and exhibited them, in passing through the village, as trophies of victory. It is said that the body was properly dressed and cooked in a large pot, and that the flesh was devoured with much relish at the public festival amidst universal merriment and rejoicing of the assembled multitude.[14]

There are many aspects of cannibal behavior that are softened by less aggressive, even affectionate, emotions. It is important to establish, however, that the cannibal act is deeply embedded in basic human aggressive attitudes. The eating of someone who is an enemy carries with it the feeling of ultimate satisfaction of aggression. Therefore, the study of cannibalism can be a most rewarding venture, since it will help us understand the nature of all institutionalized social aggression.

A fundamental psychological attitude that the cannibal maintains toward his own cannibalism is one of *ambivalence*, that is, the psychological state of both wanting and not wanting to have a certain desire—the state of entertaining contradictory feelings about setting into motion actions that would accomplish that desire. Ambivalence can result from two

14. A. Featherman, *Social History of the Races of Mankind*, vol. 3 (London: Trübner & Co., 1881–91), p. 59.

sources; fear is one—fear that the acting out of certain pleasurable wishes will bring punishment and retribution. This retribution can come from an external source or it can come from an inner psychological source. If the perception of the possibilities of punishment is strong enough, it will result in an ambivalent attitude toward the act.

The second source of ambivalence lies in desiring two contradictory things, so that the more done of one, the less that can be done of the other. This kind of ambivalence results from the desire to do two mutually exclusive things. The ambivalence of the cannibal toward his own cannibalism arises from both these sources.

One way of dealing with ambivalent or contradictory attitudes is to designate certain people in the culture to perform specific activities and to prohibit all others from doing so. If there exists both the desire to abandon cannibal behavior and the desire to continue it, one resolution of this conflict is to assign certain members of the culture to engage in cannibal behavior while the others look on from a safe distance. When we observe a society behaving in such a manner, we may justly ask why all members of the tribe do not enjoy the eating of human flesh, if some take such pleasure in it. Or, why don't all cease doing it, if there is something "wrong" with it? The answer clearly is that the society is ambivalent in its attitude. Within its institutionalized norms, there is a split. The solution is to split the society; some do and some do not.

The Kwakiutl Indians, of northwest North America, allowed cannibal activity only to those who were members of the cannibal society. The tribe was divided into various societies who performed dances and other rituals for the tribe as a whole during the period of winter ceremonials; one of the most important and prestigious of these was the cannibal society. During the course of their performance, the members of the cannibal society devoured human flesh. No other acts of cannibalism were performed by the Kwakiutl except these specific and restricted acts.

A member of the Kwakiutl cannibal society was called *hā'mats'a* and was possessed of a violent desire to eat human flesh. After an initiation period of three or four months during which he was secluded in the woods, the *hā'mats'a* reappeared near the village, whistling sharply and crying out, "*hāp, hāp, hāp*" ("eating, eating, eating"). He had come to fetch his *k·ī'nglaLala,* a female relative whose job it was to procure food for him to eat. He rushed about wildly, biting pieces of flesh out of the arms and chests of people. His main cannibal food consisted of the corpses of members of the tribe that had been preserved for months and the bodies of slaves who were killed for his pleasure. "A female slave was asked to dance for the *hā'mats'a.* Before she began dancing she said: 'Do not get hungry, do not eat me.' She had hardly said so when her master, who was standing behind her, split her skull with an axe. She was eaten by the *hā'mats'a.*"[15]

The noncannibal members of the tribe participated eagerly in the activities of the *hā'mats'a.* When a slave was killed for the delectation of the *hā'mats'a,* the body of the slave was cut up by others, and the Bear Dancers (who were not cannibals) took up the flesh, held it like bears and growled as they gave it, in turn, to each *hā'mats'a* to devour.[16] It was the job of one group to soothe and restrain the frantic cannibal, whereas the members of the Kuekutsa societies endeavored to excite his passion. They offered him a kettle of food and then upset it as soon as it began to boil. The *hā'mats'a* was traditionally excited by the mention of certain words, such as *ghost* or *skulls* or *head cut off;* these words were deliberately used in songs in his presence. When the cannibal entered a frenzied state, the Fool Dancers shut the doors to prevent escape of those inside, and the *hā'mats'a* ran around biting whomever he could.[17]

The noncannibal members of the tribe participated very closely in the cannibal activities of the *hā'mats'a.* Since they were deeply involved in assisting the cannibal tribesman, and

15. Franz Boas, *The Social Organization and the Secret Societies of the Kwakiutl Indians* (Washington, D.C.: Washington Govt. Printing Office, 1879), pp. 439–440.
16. Ibid., p. 439.
17. J. G. Frazer, *Totemism and Exogamy,* vol. 3 (London: Macmillan & Co., 1910), p. 526.

since cannibalism was highly respectable, why then didn't all members of the tribe engage in the eating of human flesh? Why does any culture give up the eating of human flesh? Civilized people continue to kill other civilized people; why have they ceased to be cannibals?

The ambivalence instrinsic to cannibal behavior is reflected in the fact that almost all cannibal activity is circumscribed by forms of ritual that have as their purpose the integration of cannibalistic acts into the normal activities of the tribe. Freud asserts in *Totem and Taboo* that all acts of taboo are the result of an attempt to deal with an inherent ambivalence: toward incest or toward the death of someone loved. In the case of the cannibal society of the Kwakiutl, the *hā'mats'a*'s activities, after he had indulged his desire to eat human flesh, were completely circumscribed by restrictions and taboos.

> After they have bitten people and particularly after they have devoured slaves and corpses, the cannibals have to observe many stringent rules before they are allowed to mix freely with other people. As soon as they have eaten a corpse, they swallow great quantities of salt water to make them vomit. The bones of the body which they have devoured are preserved for four months. . . . The cannibals may not go out of the house by the ordinary door, but must always use the secret door in the rear of the house. . . . When they go back to the house they must raise their feet four times before they enter it. With the fourth step they actually pass the door and go in right foot first. In the doorway they turn four times and walk slowly into the house. They are not allowed to look back.
>
> Further, for four months after eating human flesh the cannibal uses a spoon, dish, and kettle of his own, which are afterwards thrown away. Before taking water out of a bucket or a brook, he must dip his cup thrice into the water, and he may not take more than four mouthfuls at a time. He must carry the wing bone of an eagle and drink through it, as his lips may not touch the brim of his cup. . . . For sixteen days after partaking of human flesh he may not eat any warm food, and for four months he is not allowed to blow

> hot food in order to cool it. For a whole year he may not touch his wife, nor gamble, nor work. When the dancing season is over, he feigns to have forgotten the ordinary ways of man and has to learn everything anew. He acts as though he were very hungry all the time.[18]

The restricted behavior demanded of the cannibal suggests that of a man doing penance for sinful acts, even though the word *sinful* is never an accurate description of primitive behavior. If the society felt that there was absolutely nothing wrong with eating human flesh, it would not have been necessary to treat the *hā'mats'a* as if he were a criminal who had trespassed the law and was required to do penance. The ambivalence of the Kwakiutl toward cannibalism is demonstrated by the fact that all did not do it, only some; and those who did it were treated like outcasts for a prescribed time before they could return to the normal activities of the tribe.

Among tribes whose cannibalism is not restricted to selected members, cannibal activity is also completely surrounded by ritual activity. Examining ritual activities involved with cannibal behavior tells us much about the role of aggression within the religious experience.

The Flesh Tabooed to the Slayer

If the killing and eating of human flesh is a simple, one-dimensional human activity, why is it that the man who does the killing is forbidden the pleasure of consuming the flesh in many instances? Why is it that others are allowed to eat the fruits of his victory and he is not?

> I eat a hand of Aipura; I did not eat Laura, because I had killed her. It is not our custom to eat a person whom you have killed. If, after killing a man, you sit on a coconut, with a coconut under each heel, and get your daughter to boil the man's heart, you may drink the water in which the heart is boiled, and may eat a little of the heart, but you must be

18. Ibid., p. 525–526.

sitting on the coconuts all the time. Otherwise, you must not eat any part of a person whom you have killed yourself.[19]

In Orokaiva, New Guinea, the taboo on the flesh of the slain applied to the slayer, his father and mother, and his nearest relatives. If any of these were foolish enough to break this taboo, their genitalia would swell, their joints grow crooked, and their heads turn bald. The slayer removed his perineal band immediately after the murder and waited until he returned home to put on a new and different one; this was a precaution against elephantiasis of the scrotum. He was equally careful not to shoulder the weapon used because this act could result in a distorted shoulder joint. Having observed various restrictions concerned with eating and sexual intercourse, the slayer returned to ordinary existence after eating the *suna,* a purificatory stew. Among the Binandele, the slayer climbed a small tree swarming with large and aggressive green ants. While he sat in the fork of the tree, branches were broken and laid over him, so that he was thoroughly bitten. Only then might he climb down, eat the *suna,* and resume ordinary life.[20] It is a strange way to treat a hero, unless there is something inherently contradictory in this kind of heroism.

The split between slaying and eating is sometimes further extended into restrictions forbidding the man who captures the victim to slay him. There is a danger perceived by the cannibal in the whole process of capturing, killing, and eating. One method of dealing with this danger is to spread the liability by giving different functions to different people. Williams reports about New Guinea that the man who captures the victim receives the honor and the glory, but the actual dispatching of the victim belongs to someone else. This latter person not only kills the captive but also enjoys the privilege of biting off the victim's nose. He is called the *poki vake,* "nose man."[21]

19. J. H. P. Murray, *Papua, or British New Guinea* (New York: C. Scribner's Sons, 1912), p. 180.
20. Williams, *Orokaiva Society,* pp. 174–175.
21. F. E. Williams, *The Natives of the Purari Delta* (Port Moresby: Government Printer, 1924), p. 188.

Ritual Protection of the Slayer

A great many tribes regard the slayer of the cannibal victim as being in great danger, and rituals are performed to ward it off. The danger does not come from any real threat. We may surmise that the slayer is not particularly vulnerable to revenge attacks from the enemy tribe, since the ritual that is performed does not protect the slayer from harm from that quarter. The danger has a supernatural source. Sometimes it is spoken of as the dead man's ghost—an answer given to the question of what threatens the slayer, but not really an explanation.

One method of protecting the slayer, as we have seen in the previous section, was to forbid the slayer to eat the human meat. Yet, this action might not be sufficient protection; therefore:

> the actual killer or captor of the man who was to be eaten would go straight to his own hut, and stay there for about a month, living on roast taro and hot coconut milk; his wife would continue to share his hut, but must for that period sleep apart from him. He remains thus isolated in his hut because he is afraid of the "blood" of the dead man, and it is for this reason that he does not join his fellow warriors in partaking of the flesh. For if he were to do this, he believes his belly would become "full of blood" and he would promptly die.[22]

In Maori, the war party was met outside the village by the priestesses, who danced a *whaka-tama* ("dance of derision") and sang a song that asked the warriors whence they had come. They answered that they were followers of Tu the war god and had come from taking vengeance. The warriors were not allowed to mingle with the joyful people of the village until they had gone through the rite of *whaka-hoa* ("making common"). They proceeded to sit naked on the side of the stream while a naked priest offered to the god Tiki a pebble from the stream, a piece of fern root and a piece of human

22. Hogg, *Cannibalism and Human Sacrifice*, p. 140.

flesh. The principal priest took portions of the locks of hair of the warriors and offered them to the war god Tu. The high priestess was given the ear of the first man killed to eat; it was the only occasion when a woman might partake of human flesh. The hearts of the slain were roasted, a portion offered to Tu, and the rest eaten by the priests. The fighting men started dancing toward the village, bearing fern stalks in their hands to which were tied the hair of their victims. The priests shouted spells that finally removed the blood curse and left the warriors *hoa* ("common")—free from taboo and able to enter the ordinary activities of the tribe.[23]

The Ritual Celebration of Cannibalism

In the Purari Delta of New Guinea, the tribesmen were cannibalistic head-hunters. They ate the bodies of slain victims and preserved the heads, which were used for ritual purposes. One of the most important rituals was the *Gopi* ceremony, where the taking of heads and the eating of the flesh played a crucial part. Young men were initiated into the Gopi ceremony, and Williams reports that in earlier cannibal times a fresh head had to be furnished for each initiate. He did not have to secure the head himself but could buy it for the price of a pig.

In cannibal times, strangers would be eaten whenever the opportunity presented itself, but the *dakea,* or "organized expedition," only took place when a Gopi ceremony was being planned and fresh heads were needed. Villages conveniently situated for mutual raiding would keep a feud vigorous and healthy, but a village did not rush to immediate revenge. Its anger was contained until the planning for the next ceremony demanded an organized expedition to process the necessary heads.[24]

On the Amazon, the ritual celebration of the cannibal feast provided a great occasion for the outpouring of emotion.

23. E. Tregear, *The Maori Race* (Wanganui, New Zealand: A. D. Willis, 1904), p. 363.
24. Williams, *Natives of the Purari Delta,* pp. 107, 180–181.

> But the cannibal ritual of insult is not the end. When the orgy of blood and gluttony is over, the warrors must dance. The music is chiefly that of the drums and their gloomy rolling. . . . the warriors lurch portentously, drunk already with victory and excited by dancing. They break apart frequently to stir the great troughs of liquor with the forearms of their dead enemies, and to quaff deep calabashes full of drink. Then they stagger back to the wild intoxication of the dance. Their songs become shrieks, demoniacal, hellish. For eight days this horrible dance of triumph continues.[25]

The Ritual Qualification of Eating

Those acquainted with the determined quality of primitive thought would expect there to be a great many rules concerning the eating of the cannibal victim. In some cases, women are forbidden to eat human flesh; in others, the women partake as freely as the men. Occasionally, only particular women can participate, for example, a priestess, the chief's wife, or the widow of the slain warrior who is being revenged. Old people who have lost many of their teeth are sometimes forbidden human flesh.

The rules vary for children. Some tribes only allow human flesh to boys after they have been initiated; others start the education for cannibalism very young, giving small bits to small mouths. In one case, the children are told that it is pig's flesh because they might reject it if they knew they were eating human flesh.

The whole body may be eaten, or just certain parts; they may include the heart, the liver, the blood, the hands, the flesh of the skull, the genitalia. Conversely, certain parts of the body may be forbidden. There is no consistency or even special trend among tribes with respect to these regulations. The only consistent rule is that there must be some ritual sanction about what parts can be eaten and what cannot, and by whom; there is very little room for individual option. This restriction of the manner in which the flesh is eaten and the

25. Thomas Whiffen, *The North-West Amazons* (London: Constable and Company, Ltd., 1915), p. 204.

determination of what parts are eaten or forbidden is another indication of the ritual aspects that surround cannibalism.

Even when many different parts of the body are eaten, a certain part may be preferred; it tastes better or else it is a sign of honor to eat it. The soles of the feet, the palms of the hands, the breast of a woman, the penis of a man, the heart, the liver—all of these are mentioned by one tribe or another as the preferred morsels. But again, there is no pattern of preference among tribes.

Taking the Name of the Victim

One practice, which was found in New Guinea, is very interesting in that it throws light on the psychological origin of cannibalism. We can easily comprehend the eating of an enemy one hates, out of intense anger; we can also recognize that if such an enemy is a brave warrior we take away and absorb his strength and bravery in the process of eating him. We take away his courage, but we destroy him. But why take his name? Presumably, he is someone detested and hated whose flesh is to find its grave in his slayer's stomach. To assume his name, to be called by that name in the future, is truly to incorporate that person into oneself. This incorporation is done with someone who is a hated enemy. It is another indication that the expression and satisfaction of aggression is something more than a one-dimensional experience.

Williams suggests that the practice of taking the name of the cannibal's victim is very common. When a warrior has slain an enemy, he takes his name and is known by it for the rest of his life. He does not entirely abandon his original name, which may still be used occasionally by immediate friends. If he succeeds in killing subsequent victims, he does not assume their names, but continues to be known by the name of the first victim. A warrior would not hesitate to kill a woman, but he would not assume her name; the slayer has been known to give the name of his woman victim to his infant daughter. It is also common to bestow the victim's name on one's child born after the killing—a strange mixture of honor and hatred.[26] Perhaps all hatred is mixed with such honor.

In this chapter, I have attempted to establish three important ideas: first, cannibalism is a direct expression of human aggression; second, the attitude of human beings toward their own cannibalism is ambivalent; third, cannibalism takes place under the umbrella of ritual. These three ideas are intimately related to each other. If we can successfully weave the threads together, we may discover relationships of aggression, ambivalence, and religion that may, in fact, be true for all societies.

26. Williams, *Orokaiva Society*, pp. 175–176.

Affectionate

2

Cannibalism

In the preceding chapter, the existence of ambivalent attitudes in all cannibal behavior was one subject examined. The discussion may be broadened to include aggressive behavior in general, not merely cannibal activity. As we mentioned earlier, the fear of retribution is certainly a factor in making a person reluctant to satisfy an aggressive feeling; and there may be inhibition in the feeling, either conscious or unconscious, that to satisfy a specific aggressive urge is wrong. Conscience may assert its authority and tell us not to do the thing we wish done; it may, indeed, make cowards of us all, if by cowardice we mean a hesitation to proceed with an aggressive desire. But it may also be true that there is something *affectionate* in all expressions of aggression; we may have feelings of affection toward the object of aggression, and these feelings may be the cause of an inherent ambivalence in all aggressive acts.

A review of many descriptions of cannibalism yields the striking impression that a large number of cannibalistic acts can most accurately be described as affectionate cannibalism. This activity consists of eating the bodies or parts of the bodies of dead kinsmen who have not been killed for that purpose but who have died a normal death. Eating the dead is certainly cannibalism, but eating dead kinsmen is a profoundly different form of cannibalism from the aggressive eating of victims outside the clan described in the previous chapter.

There is a handful of reports of people within a cannibal society who have killed and eaten near relatives. Some men have eaten their wives; some women have eaten their own or other's children. In some of these cases, we have a right to doubt the accuracy of the reports. For our purposes, it makes no difference whether these stories are true or not because they represent unique and aberrational behavior; they are not typical of any tribe. No society has institutionalized, regularized, or ritualized this kind of action. In our society, a person in a psychotic state may kill members of his family; in a cannibal society such a person might then proceed to eat the victim. Such behavior, however, is not normative for any society, and we are concerned here with normative cannibal activity.

There are reported cases of old people having been killed and their bodies eaten when these people were approaching death. Even here, however, the killing and eating were done by people outside the kin. In northern Nigeria, "old men were commonly eaten by the Angas that their spirits might be dismissed from the world unweakened by disease. The members of a family would invite a neighboring quarter of the town to kill one of their old men and would even offer payment for this service. His flesh was ceremonially eaten, but his head was returned to his family, and carefully preserved in a pot, before which sacrifice and prayer were afterwards annually made."[1]

With these few exceptions: individual aberrant behavior, the small number of recorded cases of killing of old people, and the unusual behavior of the Leopard society mentioned in the last chapter, one can generalize that no member of a clan or tribe is killed in order that his or her body may be eaten. All killing for the purpose of cannibal satisfaction is done *outside* the tribe.

Kinsmen and relatives who died a normal death might be eaten as part of the funeral ritual; this eating of the dead was

1. C. K. Meek, *The Northern Tribes of Nigeria*, vol. 2 (Oxford: Clarendon Press, 1925), pp. 56–57.

engaged in by tribes who did not practice the more aggressive forms of cannibalism. There were tribesmen who ate their dead relatives and nobody else. Some tribes practiced both of these forms of cannibalism. Among the Kwakiutl, who restricted cannibalism to the *hā'mats'a* society, the corpses of dead relatives were an important item in the *hā'mats'a's* diet.

The data that we have about eating the dead comes, in an overwhelming degree, from tribes that did not practice the killing and eating of other tribesmen but engaged only in the ritual of consuming the flesh of their own dead relatives. Recourse to some of this material will indicate what is meant by the term *affectionate cannibalism.*

> There can be little doubt that the custom of disposing of the dead by eating the bodies during the days of mourning was common to all Bagesu clans. For various reasons, the custom was kept secret, and even members of the tribe were not permitted to look on during the ceremony, which was performed at night. Yet the custom was known to all, and each family was aware of what was going on, though they never sought to watch their neighbours' doings.
>
> When a man died, the body was kept in the house until evening, when the relatives who had been summoned gathered for the mourning. In some exceptional instances it took one or two days to bring the relatives together, but as a rule all was ready by the evening of the day of death and at sunset the body was carried to the nearest waste ground and deposited there. At the same time men of the clan hid themselves in different places roundabout and, as darkness deepened, they blew upon gourd horns, making a noise like the cry of jackals. The villagers said that the jackals were coming to eat the dead, and young people were warned not to go outside. When darkness had set in and it was felt to be safe to work without intrusion from inquisitive onlookers, a number of elderly women relatives of the dead man went to the place where the body lay and cut it up, carrying back the pieces they wanted to the house of mourning and leaving the remains to be devoured by wild animals.
>
> For the next three, or sometimes four, days, the relatives mourned in the house in which the death had taken place, where they cooked and ate the flesh of the dead, destroying

the bones by fire and leaving nothing. There was no purification or shaving when this mourning was ended; sometimes an ox was killed for a feast when the heir was announced, but as a rule the people simply returned to their ordinary life without any ceremony.[2]

In Australia, in the Turrbal tribes, the ritual combat of warriors following the initiation ceremonies of adolescents sometimes resulted in the death of one of the combatants. In such cases, his body was eaten by those members of his tribe who were present. A great medicine man singed the body all over with a fire stick, which caused the skin to turn copper colored. The body was then laid face downward and opened down the neck with a stone knife, turned over and slit down the front, and finally skinned. All the entrails, including the heart and lungs, were burned, and blackened sticks tied with grass were laid over the burial place. The medicine man cut off pieces of the flesh and threw it to the several groups sitting round, who cooked it and ate it. The medicine men rubbed the fat over their own bodies. When asked why they did all this, the people of the tribe replied that "they knew him and were fond of him, and they now knew where he was, and his flesh would not stink. His mother carried the skin and bones for months with her, and when one tribal group met another, the old woman would lift the Opposum rug off the skin, which was placed in a 'humpy' (hut). . . ."[3]

Among the tribes around Mayborough in Queensland, a man killed in such a ceremonial fight was skinned by his father, if alive, or by his father's brother or some other older man. The fat on the kidneys was rubbed on the spears of his relatives, and the kidneys themselves were impaled on the points of two spears. This was believed to make the spears extremely deadly when thrown. The dead man was eaten, so they said, in order that his virtues as a warrior might go into those who swallowed the flesh.[4]

2. John Roscoe, *The Bagesu and Other Tribes of the Uganda Protectorate* (Cambridge: At the University Press, 1924), p. 40.
3. A. W. Howitt, *The Native Tribes of South-East Australia* (London: Macmillan & Co., 1904), pp. 752–753.
4. Ibid., p. 753.

In most cases, the reason given for eating dead kinsmen was that some benefit would accrue to the tribe from this cannibal act. In the village of Iwi in New Guinea, they ate the penis of a man who had been killed, in order to gain strength.[5] Also in New Guinea, in the village of Togo, after the flesh had been eaten, some of the bones of the deceased were buried in the garden to make it prolific; other bones were burnt and the residue rubbed on the trunks of fruit trees to make them more productive.[6] On the Amazon, the Tariánas and Tucános drank a mixture of liquid and the powdered remains of the burnt corpse so that the virtues of the deceased might pass into the drinkers.[7] The Tangara in Australia carried the remains of the deceased in a bag; whenever they felt sorrow for the dead, they cut off a piece of flesh and ate it.[8] Of other tribes, Howitt remarks, "The aborigines said that the body was eaten, with no desire to gratify or appease the appetite, but only as a symbol of respect and regret to the dead." Even when a man had killed a warrior of another tribe, he might preserve the fat for the purpose of avoiding a blood feud. When he was called to account by the relatives of the dead man, he gave them some of the fat to eat, and this had the effect of pacifying them; they were even grateful to him and no longer felt sad or wept.[9]

These acts of affectionate cannibalism are all parts of the funeral rituals of the tribes involved. The emotional aspects of these acts are very similar to our own feelings toward dead relatives: affection, sorrow, and the desire to preserve and remember the virtues of the deceased. The one aspect of the ceremony that is most foreign to us is that of eating the flesh of the dead person. The emotional ambiance of this kind of cannibalism seems profoundly different from the war-revenge-sadism cannibalism that we have previously looked at. And yet, in both situations human flesh is consumed by

5. J. H. P. Murray, *Papua, or British New Guinea*, p. 218.
6. E. Baxter Riley, *Among Papuan Headhunters* (London: Seeley, Service & Co., Ltd., 1925), p. 174.
7. A. R. Wallace, *Travels on the Amazon* (Ward Lock, 1853), p. 489.
8. Howitt, *Native Tribes of South-East Australia*, pp. 444–450.
9. Ibid., pp. 449, 458.

other humans. One cannot help feeling that there is some connection between these two forms of behavior.

The simplistic answer to the question why certain people eat dead relatives is that it satisfies a need. Conversely, several reasons may be given why other people refrain from this practice: they may have no desire to eat the dead; they may have the desire but it is either very weak and easily put away, or else it is repressed, for any number of reasons, and is not satisfied; the third possibility is that they may have the desire, but it is satisfied in a symbolic way. Instead of actually eating the body of the deceased, they may do something which is, psychologically considered, very close to a cannibal act but is not the thing itself. If the symbolic gratification really satisfies the cannibalistic desire, then the emotional gain is the same as if the act were literally performed. Such symbolic gratification, when it does its job adequately, can be described as sublimated satisfaction. To sublimate the desire to eat the flesh of a dead kinsman is to do something that symbolizes such consumption and gives one the emotional gratification that is derived from the actual act itself, without literally consuming the flesh.

The undeveloped ego of the small child reacts to all undesired separation from the sources of love and physical sustenance as if it were abandonment. A substantial part of the terror of death—that final, irreversible separation—consists of the fact that all people react to it as abandonment. When someone who has been emotionally very important in one's life dies, especially if that person has provided psychological support, one has to deal with intense, anxious feelings of separation. The intensity of these feelings and the finality of the separation force the psyche to retreat to a very early time of life, a time when separation and the sense of abandonment are congruent.

The small child does not respond to the frustrations of separation and abandonment with a fatalistic passivity. It becomes uncontrollably angry. Only the reappearance of the source of love and food puts an end to this anger. This automatic response of anger stays with us throughout life. We become angry when we are thwarted in our desire for something or someone; we become angry when we are faced with a situation of undesired separation; we become most angry when we feel that we are being abandoned. When someone dies and leaves us behind, we cannot help but feel that we have been abandoned; we cannot react to this situation without intense feelings of anger at the person who has thus left us deprived of his or her support. This is not to say that we are necessarily conscious of these feelings of anger; the likelihood is that our feelings of anger will be repressed and, therefore, remain unconscious.

One way the small child has of simultaneously satisfying its anger and its desire for physical and psychological sustenance is to *orally incorporate* the source of the frustration and aggression. In the deep recesses of its imagination, the child can entertain the idea of eating the person who has abandoned it. This imaginative act of oral incorporation has both an affectionate and an aggressive dimension: affectionate because the needs of psychological and physical sustenance seek satisfaction in the manner in which the child has always satisfied these needs—by an oral act; aggressive because the demands of anger are satisfied by eating the cause of that anger.

The undeveloped imagination of the cannibal does not deal very adequately with metaphorical usage. He is compelled to take the urge for oral incorporation literally. He eats the person who, by dying, has abandoned him. This act of literal oral incorporation has an affectionate and an aggressive dimension. As with all of us, the aggressive aspects of the situation are not conscious with the cannibal; he gives voice only to the affectionate feelings involved in this action.

As the imagination develops, the need for literal implementation of psychic urges decreases. The aggressive needs may be satisfied in a symbolic way. New rituals are invented which satisfy, in a sublimated form, the desires for oral incorporation. As the sublimation process develops, the actual ritual performed gets further and further away from the original psychic desire—to maintain the continued presence of the person who has abandoned one by eating his flesh.

One mode of sublimating the desire to eat the corpse is to place an animal (a legitimate food) in close connection with the corpse (an illegitimate food) and then proceed to eat the animal, leaving the corpse alone. "When a man died his widow or widows slept beside the body for two days before it was buried. They threw all kinds of grain upon the body in the grave and also threw in the first earth. A cow or bull was killed and the body wrapped in the skin, while the meat was eaten by the mourners during the days of mourning. The grave was dug in the house where the man had died and mourning went on for five days, the people wailing each morning at four o'clock. On the third day a second cow was killed and eaten by the mourners, and on the fifth day they departed to their own homes."[10]

On the island of Vate in the New Hebrides, old people were put to death by burying them alive. A hole was dug, and the victim was placed in it with a live pig tied to each arm. Before the grave was closed, the cords were cut, and the pigs removed, killed, and served at the funeral feast.[11]

An even more sublimated mode of expression—one that requires no form of eating whatsoever and that preserves a continuing relationship with the dead body—is the custom of preserving and wearing the bones of the corpse. These mementos of the deceased are preserved by the relatives clearly out of feelings of affection. This method of maintaining contact with the body of the deceased preserves an infantile concept of affection. It relates, therefore, to the same psychological motive that prompts other peoples to actually eat the flesh of the dead.

At Iwa in Melanesia, the corpse of a man was buried, and subsequently the grave was opened by the man's widow and his relatives. They removed the skull, the bones of the forearm, the fibula, and the cervical vertebrae; these were brought to the beach and cleaned. The widow and children took the skull to their house and the other relatives took the long bones and made them into spatulas that were used

10. Roscoe, *Bagesu and Other Tribes*, p. 95.
11. Edwin Sidney Hartland, *The Legend of Perseus*, vol. 2 (London: David Nutt, 1895), p. 287.

ceremonially. The jaw bone of the dead man was worn by the widow and her brothers; the vertebrae and phalanges were worn by her children.[12]

In Papua, a long and elaborate ceremony was performed on the skull of the deceased. It was washed, rubbed with sweet-smelling leaves, and elaborately decorated. Small red and black berries served for eye decorations, while pieces of pearl shell replaced the eyes themselves; a false nose was constructed of beeswax. After the beautification of the skull was complete, a great feast and dance took place. The skull was placed in an empty spot between heaps of food, in front of the widow or the father and mother. After much weeping and wailing, the wife or parents took the skull home, where it was placed in a basket that hung from one of the rafters of the house. When the widow went to the garden, she took the basket with her. Should she go on a trip of several days, the basket was left in the care of an old woman, who received some produce for her trouble.[13]

The process of sublimation is a continuing one. The custom of wearing a part of the dead body is itself capable of sublimation, so that we find evidence of it in civilized peoples: the preservation of the ashes of the deceased in an accessible place or the wearing of a lock of hair of the departed person. Hartland sums up this mode of behavior: "The motive that prompts an English mother to wear in a brooch a lock of hair and the likeness of the darling she will see no more on earth is the same as induces a Friendly Islander to pass a braid of the hair of his dead kinsman through his own ear, and to wear it there for the rest of his life. It is the same as leads a Mosquitto widow to carry about her husband's bones and to sleep with them. Consciously or unconsciously the idea at the root of these and similar practices is that of sacramental communion with the dead."[14]

Although the desire for sacramental communion is the same for the English mother and the Mosquitto widow, the

12. Seligmann, *Melanesians of British New Guinea*, pp. 721–722.
13. Riley, *Among Papuan Headhunters*, pp. 171–173.
14. Hartland, *Legend of Perseus*, p. 320.

forms that the communions take are profoundly different. The lock of hair in a brooch is almost a metaphor—certainly a highly refined symbolic expression—of the love experienced between the mother and the child; it is almost impossible to see any connection here with aggressive feelings. Bones of a corpse are a different matter: bones are the residue of a meal; daily experience reinforces this symbolic connection. Carrying about the bones of a dead husband is a form of communion much closer to the original sacramental communion with the dead—the ritual of actually eating the flesh from the corpse. To carry the bones of a dead husband about is to be constantly reminded not only of the affection that was felt for the husband when he was alive but also of the feelings of anger that were felt when he died and permanently abandoned those who were still living. The more sublimated the forms of sacramental communion, the greater is the affectionate dimension and the less is the aggressive dimension present in the ritual act.

If we leave the customs of primitive peoples and look at funeral rituals that have been practiced in modern Europe, it is clear that a sublimated form of eating the corpse has persisted down to very recent times. In Albania, cakes of boiled wheat were carried in the funeral procession and eaten by the mourners upon the grave as soon as it was filled up. In some villages, the cakes were prepared so as to bear the image of the dead. They were broken and eaten upon the tomb immediately after interment, each mourner calling on God to give rest to the corpse. In the highlands of Bavaria, the corpse was laid out in a room in the house. Corpse cakes called *Leichen-nudelh* were prepared from a dough that had been left to rise on the dead body. The funeral guests ate these cakes so that the virtues and advantages of the departed might be preserved within the living kinspeople.[15]

In the custom of the wake, a great deal of drinking of alcoholic beverages goes on in the intimate presence of the corpse. In the time of Charles II, an observer at a funeral of a

15. Ibid., pp. 288–289, 296–297.

nobleman noted that a large pot of wine was placed on the coffin, out of which the mourners drank to the eternal rest of the deceased, while the minister gave his funeral oration.[16]

In the same manner that primitive peoples place a cow or pig in close proximity to the corpse and subsequently eat the animal and not the corpse, so in these cases from modern Europe, some food or drink is magically identified with the dead body before being ingested by the mourners. The unconscious psychic desire to eat the body of the dead is satisfied in a sublimated way.

With the development of the notion of sin, a notion foreign to almost all primitive peoples, the idea developed that the sins of the departed could be washed away by an act of eating. In Wales and on the Welsh border, being a sin-eater developed into an occupation.

> "One of them I remember lived in a cottage on Rasse-highway. (He was a long, lean, ugly lamentable poor raskal.) The manner was that when the corpse was brought out of the house and layd on the Biere, a Loafe of bread was brought out and delivered to the Sinne-eater over the corpse, as also a Mazor-bowle of maple (Gossips bowle) full of beer, wch he was to drinke up, and sixpence in money, in consideration whereof he took upon him (ipso facto) all the Sinnes of the Defunct, and freed him (or her) from walking after they were dead."

At a Hindu funeral in Sindh, the relatives returned to the house and offered the couch, bedding, and some clothes of the deceased to a Karnigar, a low caste-man, who was in attendance. In order to obtain these items, he had to eat a certain sweetmeat prepared for the occasion; if he did not, it was believed that the ghost of the dead man would haunt the place.[17]

Freud shows that within the unconscious and in the manifest content of dreams a desire is very readily transformed into its opposite; he never gives reasons why this is so. In the

16. Ibid., p. 298.
17. Ibid., pp. 194, 295–296.

study of funeral practices that relate to cannibalism, we find the same thing to be true. Certain peoples eat the bodies of their deceased kinspeople out of *affection;* other peoples make offerings to the dead of parts of their own bodies as a sign of mourning and concern for the deceased. If the relatives of a dead person cut off a finger joint or spill their blood on the face of the corpse,[18] it is logical to assume, knowing what we know about the practice of eating the corpse, that these relatives are offering parts of their own bodies to the deceased so that they may be eaten by him. Among the Orang Sakei in eastern Sumatra, the kinsfolk at a funeral make crosscuts on their heads with knives and drop the blood on the face of the corpse. Some people have done this so often that they have lost much of the hair on their heads. "They have indeed, in the words of the Deuteronomist, made a baldness between their eyes for the dead."[19]

These rituals of offering parts of one's own body to the dead are themselves capable of development into more sublimated forms. Instead of actually offering blood or a finger joint, one can mutilate one's body as a sign of grief, seemingly with no connection with the corpse. The Bible prohibits all such bodily mutilations but allows one to put ashes on oneself in a symbolic, sublimated mutilation. When ashes and sackcloth are considered too primitive, people can wear something black or cut their clothing instead of their bodies, as is still done today. All such acts are done for the sake of establishing and maintaining communion with the dead. The psychological and cultural antecedent of these rituals is the act of affectionate cannibalism—eating the body of the dead.

When we observe with Freud that a desire can readily be translated into its opposite, when we observe that some primitive peoples eat their dead while others offer their own bodies to be eaten—when we try to analyze these phenomena, we get closer to understanding a quality inherent in all cannibalism: ambivalence. The desire to eat someone and

18. Ibid., pp. 321–324.
19. Ibid., p. 322.

the desire to be eaten by someone lie so close together in the psyche that we cannot express the one without having to deal, at the same time, with the other. There is a basic polarization in anthropophagy between affection and aggression. It may very well be that lying in back of this is a more basic ambivalence—whether to eat or to be eaten.

The Sublimation of

3

Aggressive Cannibalism: Head-Hunting

The Jibaro Indians inhabited the lands around the Rivers Pastaza, Morena, and Upano-Santiago in South America—lands that include parts of Ecuador and Peru. The Jibaro were divided into a number of small tribes generally hostile to one another. They were said to have been the most warlike of any Indian tribe in South America. The primary aim of the education of young boys was to teach them to be fierce warriors; wars of extermination between tribes were incessant.

> The Indian does not content himself with merely killing his enemy. He wants to shed as much blood as possible and delights in mutilating the body of the slain enemy, being especially anxious to secure his head. The scene of battle between Jibaro Indians, therefore, generally appears a dreadful spectacle of savage lust of destruction and thirst for blood. . . .
>
> Along the back side of the head, from the apex downward, a long cut is made with a knife, whereupon the scalp and the skin of the face is slowly and carefully drawn off from the skull, in much the same way as is done with the hides of animals for stuffing. The skinning of the face is said to be the most difficult part of this work, for here the skin does not loosen by merely drawing it off, but has to be cut from

> the flesh with a sharp knife. The skull and all fleshy parts that adhere to it are thrown away and the scalp obtained is further prepared.[1]

The aggressive actions of the Jibaro seem to us to be as savage and as gruesome as any of the cannibal behavior that we have previously discussed. The Jibaro warrior seems to be capable, in the pursuit of revenge, of any atrocity. And yet, there is one thing that he is not capable of doing—there is one thing that he does not do to debase his enemy and satisfy his revenge lust—he does not eat any part of the bodies of those he has savagely slain.

The Jibaro, with his constant blood lust and wars of revenge and his elaborate preservation of the heads of the slain, does not strike us as being too civilized for such activity. It would not be surprising if Karsten informed us that the heads are preserved as trophies, and the rest of the body is eaten in a joyous cannibal feast. When the Jibaro speaks of an enemy whom he hates with a particular intensity, he says *Youtahei* ("I will eat him!")[2] In point of fact, however, he does not eat the enemy; he merely kills him, cuts off the head, and preserves it as a trophy. Why does the Jibaro deny himself the pleasure of these "fish of the sea"?

Head-preserving is a far better term than *head-hunting* for this kind of behavior because the preservation of the heads and their use in religious and ritual situations is the most significant aspect of this cultural activity. Head-hunting, however, is the term used by anthropologists who have studied such peoples. In all cases, the heads are not only hunted but preserved as important treasures of the tribe. There are tribes that practice both head-hunting and cannibalism; the head is preserved as a trophy and the body of the victim is eaten. Most cannibals, however, are not head-hunters; most head-hunters are not cannibals.

If we think about the occasions for head-hunting, they appear to be identical to those for cannibalism—war, re-

1. Rafael Karsten, *Blood Revenge, War, and Victory Feasts among the Jibaro Indians of Eastern Ecuador*, Bureau of American Ethnology, 79 (Washington, D.C.: Smithsonian Institution, 1923), pp. 1–2, 28, 30.
2. Ibid., p. 48.

venge, sadism, and proof of masculinity. The ritual of taboo and ceremony that surrounds head-hunting activity is almost indistinguishable from that which is intimately associated with cannibalism. On the surface, the head-hunter and the cannibal seem to be doing the same thing for the same reasons.

> It is a rule that when a victory has been attained over a foreign tribe, the heads of the slain enemies are taken. Most Jibaro warriors would consider any victory over such an enemy incomplete, and the whole war expedition more or less a failure, unless they returned with one or several head trophies. It, of course, not seldom happens that the Jibaro is able to kill an enemy but not to take his head, because his comrades are not able to secure the body and perhaps to defeat the slayers. In such a case there cannot be a real victory feast.[3]

In the Solomon Islands, it was the general practice to take heads and preserve them as signs of power and success. These heads were set out on stages or hung up under the eaves of the canoe house. When a chief had a man killed for an offense, or murdered out of revenge or hatred, or sacrificed, he added the head to his collection as a fresh sign of his power and greatness.[4] In Nigeria, a young man was considered no better than a girl, and no one would marry him until he had obtained his head in the prescribed manner and his prowess had been celebrated by a public feast. After the feast, he was considered a man and a warrior.[5]

Among the Kwakiutl:

> there was a more extreme way of meeting the affront of death. This was by head-hunting. It was in no sense retaliation upon the group which had killed the dead man. The dead relative might equally have died in bed of disease or by the hand of an enemy. The head-hunting was called "killing to wipe one's eyes," and it was a means of getting even by making another household mourn instead. When a chief's

3. Ibid., p. 28.
4. R. H. Codrington, *Melanesians*, p. 345.
5. C. K. Meek, *Northern Tribes of Nigeria*, vol. 2, p. 49.

> son died, the chief set out in his canoe. He was received in the house of a neighboring chief, and after the formalities he addressed his host, saying, "My prince has died today and you go with him." Then he killed him. In this, according to their interpretation, he acted nobly because he had not been downed, but had struck back in return.[6]

Just as the psychological and social motivations for head-hunting appear to be identical to those for cannibalism, the ritual activities associated with both are also quite similar. The slayer is subject to intense taboo, the taking of the heads is celebrated in elaborate feasts, the heads are prepared and preserved with extreme care under closely restricted rules, and the taker of the head is treated with ceremonial respect by his relatives and in-laws.

In certain tribes where head-hunting is practiced, the tribesmen do not engage in general cannibal activity, but they practice a very limited amount of cannibalism in a highly restricted way. The limited, restricted cannibal activity always takes place in connection with head-hunting. This fact is important in illustrating the very close relationship between cannibalism and head-hunting. A small dose of cannibalism becomes part of the ritual involved in head-hunting. More particularly, a small dose of cannibalism is used as protective magic to guard the safety of the head-taker, whose psychic life is endangered by the assertive act of seizing a head. In the examples that follow, it must be kept in mind that we are talking of people who do not practice cannibalism under other circumstances.

> The slayer rode round on his horse, brandishing a knife in his right hand. . . . One of the first duties of the head-getter on reaching home was to go to the house of the priest who had charge of the head-hunting rites, and receive a further dose of protective medicine consisting of two mouthfuls of palm and mahogany oil and a small piece of the flesh of the skull. . . . This rite of eating a small piece of the flesh of the skull is of peculiar interest in proving that one

6. Ruth Benedict, *Patterns of Culture* (Boston: Houghton Mifflin, 1934), p. 216.

purpose at least of cannibalism had the "religious" object of destroying the dead enemy's soul.[7]

Among the Kagaro, the protective medicine included a few drops of blood from the captured head. The warrior spent the night in the priest's house, covered with a cloth, and fumigated by the smoke of branches of certain trees. This whole process was engaged in to insure that the ghost of the slain victim would not pursue the head-taker.[8]

In several cases, the priest ate part of the flesh to protect the head-getter, but the head-getter himself did not. This flesh-eating was part of the ritual that protected the slayer. The Chawai brought all captured heads to the chief priest. The heads were boiled, the priest ate a piece of the flesh, and the skulls were then deposited in the sacred hut. The head-getter was anointed with a filthy-smelling mixture that included the intestines of a porcupine, and he remained hidden during these purification rites. Afterward, he rejoined the tribe, was treated as a hero, and drank beer with the elders.[9]

In the education of the young, a small amount of cannibalism might be permitted by tribes who engaged in no other form of eating human flesh. "A father who has been on a successful head-hunt and returned with a coveted trophy, should he have a son five or six years of age, will take a small portion of the flesh from the head, about the size of a pea, and a drop of blood, mix these with a little sago, yam or taro, or some other vegetable, make into a kind of pill, and give to the young child. . . . This is said to make boy *serawa nanito* ['fierce forever']."[10]

The Yungur denied that they preserved the heads of slain enemies, but they did preserve pieces of abdominal fat that they deposited in antelope horns and hung up in their houses as charms. If any member of the family fell ill, the horn was hung around his neck, and if this did not succeed in curing

7. C. K. Meek, *Tribal Studies in Northern Nigeria*, vol. 2 (London: Routledge and Kegan Paul, 1931), p. 70.
8. Ibid.
9. Ibid., pp. 156–157.
10. E. Baxter Riley, *Among Papuan Headhunters*, pp. 270–271.

the patient, a little of the fat was mixed with hot water and given to him to drink. It was also the Yungur's custom to lick some blood from the knife or spear that had killed a man in order to make sure that his ghost would not pursue the slayer.[11] Cannibalism was a very potent form of magic. It could give magical protection, or cure illness, or make the young boys grow into brave men.

When we see a tribe that uses cannibalism as a magical charm but does not practice general anthropophagy, we can discern a principle that is true for religion in general. It has been observed that as a religion develops some old forms will persist while others change. These old forms will have a special magical potency. A stone knife, for example, may be required for circumcision or sacrifice even when metal knives are available. The old language of the religious ritual may continue in use when it is no longer comprehensible to the worshipers, and it retains a particular magical potency because it is both old and incomprehensible. The Babylonians used the Sumerian language for ritual purposes, the Hebrews used Hebrew even when Aramaic had become the language of the people, and the Roman church used the Latin language so long for the same reason. The persistence of limited cannibal activity within a noncannibal society is an analogous development; the more ancient practice retains the greatest magical potency.

Head-hunting is an institutionalized cultural form that developed out of and replaced cannibalism. The aggressive desires that were previously satisfied by cannibal activity have been sublimated and are now satisfied by head-hunting. The relationship between anthropophagy and head-hunting illustrates the two basic components of the mechanism of sublimation. First, head-hunting continues to satisfy the aggressive needs of the individual and of the culture as a whole that cannibalism once satisfied. We need no further illustrations of war, revenge, and sadism to demonstrate that head-hunting is not a peaceful, beneficent activity. The crucial point about sublimated satisfaction is that the instinctual

11. Meek, *Tribal Studies in Northern Nigeria,* vol. 2, p. 485.

needs have not disappeared but they are now satisfied in a more symbolic, less immediate, more developed way.

Second, cannibalism is a more primitive (both psychologically and culturally) way of satisfying aggressive needs than is head-hunting. It is more primitive in that it is psychologically more fundamental and historically more ancient. In cannibalism, even though one may actually kill one's victim with a spear, one eats his body with one's mouth. Psychologically considered, the victim is not really dead until he is eaten. He is killed by the spear, but he is destroyed by being eaten. The actual physical, biological killing is not enough for the cannibal. The victim must be destroyed and incorporated into oneself. The head-hunter, on the other hand, does not eat his victim. Since there is no written law or external police force to prevent him from doing so, it is reasonable to assume that he desists from an inner psychological reason, reinforced by the authoritarian power of culture.

If head-hunting is a developmental form arising out of cannibalism, there must be, within the institutionalized form of head-hunting, certain developmental ideas, or feelings, or views of reality that cannot be discovered within the form of cannibalism. That is precisely what we do find.

The most remarkable thing about the preserved heads is the contrast between the manner in which they are obtained and the benefits that they provide for the tribe. The heads are obtained in savage, aggressive warfare, the details of which would do credit to any cannibal tribe. They are taken in a form of action that, except for one particular thing, is as savage, as gruesome, and as primitively aggressive as any form of action that human beings engage in. The one exception, of course, is that the bodies of the victims are not eaten by the victors. And yet, the benefits that accrue to the individual or to the tribe from these heads have a remarkable civilizing quality about them. The preserved heads promote the general welfare of the tribe, increase the fertility of the crops, cure sickness and disease, multiply the number of domestic animals, make a male a proper husband to his wife, promote the fertility of women, ease the passage of the spirit of a dead man to the next world, and even serve him there after death.

Karsten, who is our source of information for the head-hunting Jibaro, recognizes the dual nature of head-hunting rites and ceremonies. The hated victim and the beneficent provider are combined in the one symbolic form of the preserved head. The inherent ambivalent attitude in aggressive activity is demonstrated by the two-fold meaning that adheres to this dead and preserved skull. The symbolic form of the head and its meanings are not a contradiction but a resolution of the contradiction that lies within all aggressive action.

> Now, according to the idea of the Jibaro, it is precisely the *tsantsa* [the preserved head] which will cause the domestic animals and fields to grow and develop not only in the normal way, but with an extraordinary force. The Jibaro do not find anything contradictory in the thought that the spirit of the slain enemy on the one hand entertains feelings of hatred and revenge against his slayer and always looks for an opportunity to harm him, and on the other hand, at the same time, as it were, plays a role as his friend and adviser. The latter, it must be understood, he has become under the influence of the magical conjuration through the ceremonies performed at the feast *suamartinyu*.[12]

One cannot help but be struck by the deeply religious nature of the benefits that accrue from the preserved heads. It can be seen that there is religion in cannibal activity; I have tried to show that anthropophagy is a religious experience for the cannibal. To establish this, however, it was necessary to go behind immediate phenomena in order to discover modes of action and thought that could easily be called religious. With head-hunting and the multiple benefits that derive from the heads, however, it is more immediately clear that the action and its meaning are religious. We are well-acquainted with the fact that religion deals with problems of promoting fertility, curing sickness, easing the passage after death, and

12. Karsten, *Blood Revenge, War, and Victory Feasts,* p. 46. The feast *suamartinyu* refers to the ceremony in which the head trophy is washed in a magical solution, thereby transforming it into the slave of its captor.

so on. The religious benefits accruing to the tribe because of the preserved heads—in contrast to the seemingly irreligious activity of the cannibal—is an indication that something very important has happened in the development from cannibalism to head-hunting.

Karsten has a keen sense of the general religious nature of the preserved head and the several benefits it provides for the tribe.

> The *tsantsa* of the Jibaro Indians, thus, is not a "trophy" in the common sense of the word; not exclusively a mark of distinction or a visible proof that an enemy has been killed. The Jibaro warrior not only tries to take the life of his enemy, but above everything wants to secure control of his soul. The so-called *einsupani* is not merely a victory feast in the sense familiar to us, but at the same time, and first of all, a kind of mystery feast which, when we are able to penetrate into its real meaning, throws an interesting light not only upon the social life of these Indians in general and the ideas they connect with their wars, but also upon their, in some respects, rather far-reaching religious views. . . .
>
> The rule is, however, among the Jibaro that a warrior who has captured a head (*tsantsa*) should celebrate a feast. The head feast for the Jibaro opens the road to honor and fame, to material wealth, to new victories over enemies and a long life. It is the great mystery feast of the Jibaro Indians; as will be presently seen, it in part has a purely religious significance, inasmuch as the Jibaro through the ceremonies thereby performed believes he acquires the same benefits as most other savage peoples try to acquire by cult actions of a different kind.[13]

In certain areas of the world, the crops will not grow without the aid of human heads cut from the bodies of slain victims. The times of planting or reaping crops are the most favored times for head-hunting expeditions. The Ida in Upper Burma set forth in March, when the poppy fields were in full bloom. After the warriors secured some heads, they returned to the village where they were met with great rejoicing because the people knew that the heads would make the rice

13. Ibid., pp. 29, 89.

grow green in the depths of the valley, it would make the maize ripen in a full harvest and it would increase the white bloom of the poppy.[14]

In the Philippines, the Bantoc considered it essential that every farm have at least one new head at planting and sowing time. The raiders went out in groups of twos and threes and brought back the heads, hands, and feet of their victims. A great feast and dance followed, during which the trophies were exposed for all to triumph over. When the flesh had decayed, the skull was taken home by the man who procured it and preserved at his farm; his companions took the hands and feet.[15]

In Nigeria, the skulls were preserved by the local priest in the skull house. At every harvest, the priest offered thanks by taking out the skulls and spitting on them fragments of porridge made from the first fruits of digitaria millet.[16]

When the Jibaro wished to slaughter swine for a great feast, he hung the *tsantsa* around his neck and went into the swine yard to point out the victims to be killed. The wearing of the *tsantsa* assured that the remaining swine would increase with more than usual fecundity. The fertility of the women of the tribe was equally subject to the *tsantsa* magic and would be enhanced by the multiplicity of heads.[17] In Sarawak, all kinds of sickness, particularly smallpox, were under the influence of an evil spirit. Nothing was as effective in the propitiation of this spirit as a preserved head.[18]

Most men in all cultures are instilled with the wish to be manly. The cannibal warrior, as we have seen, enhances his masculine image with a successful cannibal hunt or battle. In social definitions of manliness, however, there is tremendous variety. The cannibal wishes to be strong, brave, and fearless; the successful procurement of human flesh to eat is the visible proof that he has succeeded. There is no indication

14. E. O. James, *Origins of Sacrifice* (London: John Murray, 1933), pp. 103–104.
15. Ibid.
16. Meek, *Tribal Studies in Northern Nigeria,* vol. 2, p. 71.
17. Karsten, *Blood Revenge, War, and Victory Feasts,* pp. 52, 81.
18. H. Ling Roth, *The Natives of Sarawak* vol. 2 (London, 1896), p. 144.

that his conception of manliness includes the capacity to be a good husband. Specifically, there is no evidence that the cannibal thinks that his capacity to procure and eat human flesh will make him a more sought-after marriage partner. The head-hunter, however, adds this sexual dimension to the benefits accruing to him for his aggressive potency.

In northern Nigeria, "Men who had taken heads in war wore two hornbill feathers in their hair. They were eagerly sought in marriage by women. For it was something for a wife to feel that if she were attacked on the farm her husband would not run and leave her."[19]

Among the head-hunters of Papua, New Guinea:

> In the old head-hunting days, if a change of daughters had been satisfactorily settled, the girls would go to their mother-in-law's house, but the future husbands would not be permitted to occupy the same quarters unless both men had taken the head of an enemy in battle. It was absolutely necessary for a young man to be possessed of such a trophy in Mawata before he could take unto himself a wife.[20]

This is not to imply that a great cannibal hunter would not have a special sexual attractiveness for women; undoubtedly, he did. But within cannibal societies, I find no evidence that this phenomenon was institutionalized to the point that acquiring human flesh for eating was a condition for marriage.

In Sarawak, the benefits to be derived from the possession of human heads were of the highest order, and the more heads a man possessed, the more benefits he could anticipate. A man of consequence could not be buried until his friends had procured a head for the ceremony. The people believed that if they possessed a man's head, that man must serve them in the next world. The more heads a man owned, the greater would be his rank in the life to come. This factor entitled the owners of the most heads to great consideration by others while still on this earth, and a man who had taken many heads walked with a proud and lofty bearing and expected others to be deferential to him. The chiefs some-

19. Meek, *Tribal Studies in Northern Nigeria*, vol. 2, p. 458.
20. Riley, *Among Papuan Headhunters*, p. 49.

times made excursions of considerable duration for the sole purpose of acquiring heads in order to assure their high level of prestige in this world and the next.[21]

One very important reason why the head-hunter can derive so many benefits from his aggressive activity—benefits not available to the cannibal—is that the head-hunter preserves a part of the body of his victim. He retains a permanent trophy of his power. The trophy itself becomes powerful. By preserving this symbol of power, the head-hunter builds a capital stock of this agency. The cannibal is like that economic society that consumes every year all that it produces: it saves nothing, it produces no capital goods, and its budget consists only of income and expenditures. When the cannibal has a need for power, he must go out and supply that need in an immediate way.

The head-hunter, on the contrary, has an ever-increasing supply of heads. He has a constant reminder of his dominant position in the world; he can see and touch and show to his neighbors this evidence of manliness; and in times of stress, he can bring out these proofs of manliness and power to aid him. The cannibal can do nothing but go out and get another victim. The head-hunter has created a *permanent* symbol of power and dominance; it is an act of imagination of which the cannibal is not capable. The cannibal insists on satisfying his vengeance and his anger immediately and to the ultimate. He must put his enemy in his stomach, destroying him forever. The stomach, however, becomes empty if you do not fill it periodically. The head-hunter's trophies do not diminish with time; they actually increase as he adds one new head to the others.

All sublimation consists of the act of substituting an imaginative for an actual satisfaction; desires that are not satisfied in an actual way may be satisfied in a symbolic way. The head-hunter does obtain much aggressive satisfaction. His cannibal desires, however, are not satisfied except in a sublimated way. Our evidence shows that the head-hunter is very close to the cannibal in his mode of action with regard

21. Roth, *Natives of Sarawak*, vol. 2, p. 141 n.

to aggression. For him, therefore, the act of cannibalism is problematic. Even though he does not do so consciously, he does make a *deliberate decision* not to eat human flesh. This decision is not easy to make or to hold to.

What the head-hunter does is to create a situation of symbolic satisfaction of his cannibal desires. The head is the most human part of the body; it is primarily by the face that we recognize people when they are alive. The skull is the most human of all the bones of the skeleton. In many cases, the head-hunter goes to great length to decorate those skulls so that their humanness is emphasized. There is no ambiguity about the fact that it is a human head that is preserved.

Having satisfied his cannibalistic desires in a symbolic way, the head-hunter is able to renounce the actual eating of human flesh. This whole process of renunciation by means of symbolic satisfaction provides the head-hunter with enormous benefits: his crops grow better, his animals multiply, the tribe itself is more fertile, disease is more amenable to cure, husbands are more attractive, servants are obtained for the next world, and the general welfare of the tribe is enhanced. The emotive and religious life of the culture takes on a depth of human feeling that is not available to the cannibal, who insists on satisfying his anger and his revenge in his mouth and in his stomach.

Sacrifice:

4

The Formal Reconciliation of Aggression and Affection

A captive youth, selected for his bravery, physical perfection, and musical accomplishments, was chosen a year in advance to impersonate Tezcatlipoca. Clad in costly garments and wreathed with flowers, he lived in regal splendor at the temple of the god with four priests and four warriors as attendants. Enjoying the freedom of the city, he wandered as he listed. Wherever he went, people prostrated themselves before him, showered him with flowers, and offered incense and sacrifices to him. Even the king bowed before the incarnation of the god. A month before the ceremony, he was married to four beautiful maidens, who bore the names of goddesses. For twenty days his brides ministered to his every desire, the great lords vied in giving feasts and dances in his honor, and every joy of earth was placed at his disposal. On the morning of the twentieth day, however, he boarded a canoe, bade farewell to his brides, and was rowed across Lake Tezcuco. Accompanied only by his eight attendants, he followed a desert trail to a small ruined temple. Stripped of his costly raiment and jewels, and clad only in a necklace of flutes, he slowly ascended the pyramid, breaking a flute at each step. Exactly at midnight, as his successor was being chosen and acclaimed in Mexico, his heart was wrenched out and offered to the god whom he had impersonated.

> . . . the well-known case recorded among the Pawnees in 1837 or 1838, of a girl of fourteen or fifteen who, after being treated with great kindness and respect for six months, was put to death on April 22nd. Two days before the sacrifice she was led from wigwam to wigwam, accompanied by the whole council of chiefs and warriors. At each she received a present of wood and paint, and after her body had been painted half red and half black, she was slowly roasted over a fire, and then shot with arrows. The chief sacrificer thereupon tore out her heart, and devoured it, the rest of her body being cut up while it was yet warm, placed in little baskets, and taken to the neighboring cornfield. There the head chief took a piece of the flesh from the basket and squeezed a drop of blood upon the newly-deposited grains of corn. The rest of the party did likewise till all the seeds had been "vitalized." They were then covered up with earth, and, according to one account, the body was made into a kind of paste which was rubbed on potatoes, beans and other seeds to fertilize them.[1]

Nowhere do we find the mysterious mixture of affection and aggression so dramatically demonstrated as we do in the institution of ritual sacrifice. Nor is it necessary to reach way back in cultural time to the Aztec or the Pawnee to observe that these two seemingly contradictory feelings may be contained within one symbolic form. The crucifixion is the primary visual religious symbol of the most influential religion in the history of the world. Central to that symbol is a god in the very process of being killed and sacrificed. The ordinary response to this great symbol combines elements of pity, sorrow, and great affection. And yet, the visual impact of the scene lies in the nails driven into the hands and feet, the thorns piercing the skin of the scalp, and the blood flowing from the gashes in the flesh.

The ritual mystery of this religion is expressed through an act of symbolic cannibalism; the flesh of the god is eaten and the blood is drunk, not actually but symbolically. And these symbolic cannibal acts are performed out of the need to

1. Murdock, *Our Primitive Contemporaries,* pp. 399–400; James, *Origins of Sacrifice,* pp. 96–97.

express and enjoy feelings of affection and communion. Communion as established with one's fellow worshipers, with the god who has been killed, with one's own past, and with the ambivalent and contradictory forces within oneself that can be reconciled within a religious form.

Sacrifice is a form of religious action that has persisted throughout all the changes religion has undergone from primitive to historical times. To my knowledge, there were no religious systems that were unfamiliar with sacrifice until very recent times. In order to understand what is really going on when a sacrificial rite is performed, we must first see that the expression of and satisfaction of deep feelings of affection and of hostility are essential to all such rites.

Some great cultural inventions of the human intellect—art, myth, history, religion, the state, science—are designated *symbolic forms* by Ernst Cassirer in his books *An Essay on Man* and *The Philosophy of Symbolic Forms*. What Cassirer does not observe is that one of the primary functions of all symbolic forms is the expression and satisfaction of contradictory, ambivalent human desires of a conscious or an unconscious nature. A symbolic form synthesizes contradictory attitudes within the psyche by giving some satisfaction to each aspect of the ambivalence, thereby denying ultimate satisfaction to either.

A neurotic symptom, Freud explains, is also the result of contradictory impulses within the psyche; this symptom gives satisfaction to both parts of ambivalent desires. The psychological process that produces symptoms is analogous to—yet is the reverse of—the process that creates symbolic form. Symbolic form may be considered a healthy symptom. Freud writes:

> Let us turn to the obsessional neuroses in the hope of learning more about the formation of symptoms. The symptoms belonging to this neurosis fall, in general, into two groups, each having an opposite trend. They are either prohibitions, precautions and expiations—that is, negative in character—or they are, on the contrary, substitutive satisfactions which often appear in a symbolic disguise. The negative, defensive group of symptoms is the older of the two; but as illness is

> prolonged, the satisfactions, which scoff at all defensive measures, gain the upper hand. The symptom-formation scores a triumph *if it succeeds in combining the prohibition with satisfaction so that what was originally a defensive command or prohibition acquires the significance of a satisfaction as well;* and in order to achieve this end it will often make use of the most ingenious associative paths. Such an achievement demonstrates the tendency of the ego to synthesize, which we have already observed. In extreme cases the patient manages to make most of his symptoms acquire, in addition to their original meaning, a directly contrary one. This is a tribute to the power of ambivalence, which, for some unknown reason, plays such a large part in obsessional neuroses.[2]

A symbolic form is also a tribute to the power of ambivalence and of the ego to synthesize. Within such a form, however, the ambivalence dealt with is not pathological but inevitable; and the synthesis built by the ego is not based on sickness but on the healthy human desire to surmount the psychological problems that all human beings face.

The words *form* or *symbolic form* may be used in connection with any cultural invention of the intellect that synthesizes a situation of ambivalence. Every cultural expression and satisfaction of aggression has an ambivalent quality about it: the religion of the head-hunter, in its totality, is a symbolic form; cannibalism equally deserves the designation of symbolic form. It is not a personal, individualized expression of aggression; it is an expression and satisfaction of aggression within a *social* context—it is the institutionalization of a psychic desire. In the process, the desire becomes *formalized,* as the ambivalent attitudes of aggression and affection are synthesized into a cultural form. Cannibalism is by no means a pre-religious or pre-formal cultural system.

There are reasons for discussing the nature of form in connection with sacrifice. Contradictory attitudes of aggression and affection toward the same object (the sacrifice

2. Sigmund Freud, *Inhibitions, Symptoms and Anxiety,* trans. Alix and James Strachey, rev. ed. (London: Hogarth, 1961), pp. 27–28, my italics.

itself) are, first of all, dramatically demonstrated. Second, sacrifice represents a smaller form within the much larger form of religion itself, and this sacrificial form has persisted throughout the tremendous changes that religion has undergone in its historical development. It is a long way from the cannibal society of Fiji to the civilized religion of nineteenth- and twentieth-century Europe. The institution of sacrifice has never been abandoned on that long journey.

The uses and benefits of sacrifice have remained constant. Sacrifice has always been used to promote fertility, ward off disease, prevent calamity, and ease the passage of the dead out of this world. The instrument sacrificed has continually changed: a man, an animal, things that grow in the ground, part of one's body, wealth, a eucharistic wafer.

It is reasonable to assume that the institution of sacrifice has its origins in cannibalism—that sacrifice is a sublimated form of cannibal behavior. Throughout the history of religion, sacrifice has been offered in these situations, among others: (1) at a funeral or other rites for the dead; (2) in religious rites that have as their object the enhancement of the general welfare of the culture; (3) to avert or to lessen the effects of a calamity; (4) at times of unusual assertive activity, such as the building of a house or a temple or a particularly important object, such as a chief's canoe; (5) in relation to kingship, especially at times when monarchial power is transferred from one individual to another; (6) to promote the fertility of crops or flocks or to insure good hunting or fishing; (7) in circumstances connected with the transference and casting out of sin (the scapegoat); and (8) to insure success in warfare.

In cannibal cultures we find that, in these circumstances, not only is a human being sacrificed, but also his flesh is eaten as part of the rite. The next developmental step is to give up the eating of human flesh but to retain the rite of human sacrifice. "The relation of human sacrifice to cannibalism is one of considerable interest, and it is noteworthy that while the northerly head-hunters were cannibals, the more southerly practiced human sacrifice. It would appear probable that the southerly tribes represent a cultural stage in advance, and that human sacrifice advanced from anthropophagy. Human flesh is precious food, for as these primitive peoples believe that the gods eat the sacrifice, what more palatable gift can be offered them than a human victim."[3]

After having catalogued the benefits to be derived from sacrifice into eight fundamental areas, it is instructive to look at each of these areas in detail, especially in those situations where human sacrifice and cannibalism are both an integral part of the rite. Such data does not establish that human sacrifice has its origins in cannibalism but it does demonstrate a very close connection between these two religious rites.

Funeral Customs and Rites for the Dead

Among the Bangalas along the Congo, when a chief or headman died, the members of certain tribes purchased slaves who were subsequently killed and eaten out of respect for the dead.[4] In southern Nigeria, after the death of a big chief or a rich woman, ten or twenty male and female slaves were beheaded, their skulls placed in the skull house, and their bodies eaten.[5]

Radin describes a situation among the Indians of South America that is of interest because it involves incorporating the intended victim into the tribe before he is killed and eaten. The victim becomes not only a revenge tribute for a warrior killed in battle but psychologically acts as a substitute for the deceased and takes his place in the tribe before he is eaten. Like the Pawnee girl or the Aztec sacrifice, it is another instance that mixes intense affection with extreme aggression.

The captive was first led to the grave of the deceased

3. Meek, *Northern Tribes of Nigeria,* vol. 2, p. 57.
4. Herbert Ward, *A Voice from the Congo* (New York: C. Scribner's Sons, 1910), p. 267.
5. P. A. Talbot, *The Peoples of Southern Nigeria* (London: Oxford University Press, 1926), p. 828.

relative of the conquerors; he was forced to clean, or "renew," these graves. Then he was led triumphantly into the village. After initial outbursts of hatred from the villagers, the prisoner practically became a member of the tribe. It might be five years before he served as an anthropophagous feast; he might never be killed. After the ceremony of cleaning the grave, the captive was always led to the hut that had been occupied by the man whose grave he had cleared off. Once there, the relatives of the dead warrior gave him the hammock, the weapons, the necklaces, and the feather ornaments of the deceased. If all the male relatives of the deceased also perished, the widows frequently married the prisoner.

In spite of this remarkable act of taking the place of the dead man, the day of reckoning more often than not did come. The prisoner was killed; a few old women rushed up to drink his blood; and the body was systematically cut up, roasted, and eaten.

The wife of the original victim approached the body, shed a few purely ceremonial tears—just the proper amount—but then quickly joined the others in an aggressive stance toward the corpse. Children were forced to touch the body and wet their hands with its blood. "You have revenged yourself on your enemy, my child," they were taught to say, "for this is the one who made you an orphan."[6] This was done to a man who might have spent five years living in the village, cohabiting with the wives of slain warriors, and who had for all practical purposes been adopted into the tribe. Affection and aggression sometimes become so intermixed in sacrifice that it is hard even to distinguish the two strands.

Religious Ceremonies to Enhance the General Welfare

On the island of Fiji, the people ate human beings on occasions when no sacrificial rite was performed, but they also

6. Paul Radin, *Indians of South America* (New York: Doubleday, 1942), p. 104.

practiced human sacrifice and ate the body. Victims for human sacrifice were obtained from outside the tribe, either by capture or by purchase from another tribe. The victim was made to sit on the ground with his feet tucked under his thighs and his hands placed in front of him. After being thoroughly tied, he was placed on red-hot stones, covered with leaves and earth, and roasted alive. The face was then blackened and the body carried to the temple of the gods and offered as a propitiatory sacrifice. Later, the body was carried out of the area of consecrated ground, cut into quarters, and distributed among the people.[7]

The Aztecs ate human flesh only on the occasion of human sacrifice, but not on all such occasions. Aztec gods craved human flesh and had to be provided with it periodically; they were divine cannibals.

> It was through human sacrifice, however, that man could provide the gods most abundantly with the refreshment they craved. Hence war—to replenish the supply of victims—became to the Aztecs a religious duty. Sometimes the captive was shot with arrows, or burned on a pyre, or decapitated and flayed, or slain in gladiatorial combat, but in general these methods were minor variations of, or preliminaries to, the usual procedure. In full view of multitudes of devout spectators, the victim solemnly ascended the steps of the pyramid and was seized at the summit by five priests. While these bent his body over backwards on a convex sacrificial stone and held his head and limbs, a sixth priest, distinguished by a scarlet mantle, with a deft stroke made an incision under the ribs, inserted his hand, and tore out the palpitating heart. This he held aloft to the sun and then tossed into a basin of copal so placed that the odor ascended into the nostrils of the idol. The priests now smeared the lips of the idol with blood, cut off the head of the victim, and tossed the body down the steps of the pyramid. The honored donor or captor of the sacrifice removed the corpse to his home, where he had the arms, legs, and thighs cooked and served in a ceremonial banquet to his kinsmen and friends.[8]

7. Hogg, *Cannibalism and Human Sacrifice*, pp. 25–26.
8. Murdock, *Our Primitive Contemporaries*, pp. 394–395.

Sacrifice to Avert Calamity

The Yoruba of southern Nigeria practiced only one act of cannibalism: when a human victim was sacrificed to promote success in warfare, they licked the blood off the headman's sword. They did practice human sacrifice on many occasions. Besides ordinary human sacrifices to make the fruit and crops plentiful, a "basket-sacrifice" was offered up in times of stress. The victim was enclosed in a long basket, which was dropped from a great height. If this did not suffice to kill the victim, he was clubbed to death. Most Yoruba towns held at least one human sacrifice a year, but this number was greatly increased in times of trouble, such as pestilence or defeat in warfare.[9]

The Edo of Benin sacrificed annually one man and one woman, one cow and one goat to Ogiwu, the god of death and lightning. In times of pestilence, such as influenza and smallpox, these sacrifices would be greatly increased.[10]

In these instances of sacrifice to avert calamity, the flesh of the human victim was not actually consumed by the worshipers. It may be that certain cultures did sacrifice humans and consume their flesh on such occasions, but such evidence is not revealed in the data available to me. On the other hand, it is possible that there is something unique about such sacrifices—that the flesh is never eaten when the sacrifice has the specific object of averting calamity. The nature of the rites illustrated from the Yoruba and the Edo are very close to other sacrificial rites where human flesh is actually consumed. It is possible that the Yoruba and Edo once ate the human bodies they sacrificed to avert calamity.

Sacrifice on Great Occasions

In Melanesia when a great house was built, the fireplace was left open, and no fire could be lighted until a man or woman

9. Talbot, *Southern Nigeria,* p. 859.
10. Ibid., p. 861.

of some other community had been killed and his or her skull smoked in the newly kindled fireplace. The body was cooked in the cannibal stone circle and eaten in the same manner as other cannibal meals.[11] Among the Maori, the heart of a human sacrifice was eaten during the house-building ceremony, at the tattooing of the lips of the chief's daughter, at the felling of a tree used for a great chief's canoe, and at the conclusion of the mourning for a chief's widow.[12] In Fiji, human victims were eaten in connection with the building of a temple or canoe. A chief would sometimes kill several men to serve as rollers to faciliate the launching of the canoe. These rollers would be cooked and eaten later as "food for the carpenters." A chief might kill a man when laying down a keel for a new canoe and might try to add one victim for each new plank. The food did not go to waste.[13]

Sacrifice in Connection with Kingship

Frazer has acquainted us with the fact that the king himself may be sacrificed for the welfare of the society; it is not surprising that the body of a king can be eaten by his successor. In Nigeria, the king of Julsum was only allowed to rule for seven years. During that period, if he fell ill, or sneezed or coughed, or fell off his horse, he might be put to death. After strangulation, the body was preserved, but his brain, kidneys, and heart were dried and eaten by his successor along with the liquid that exuded from his body after his decease.[14]

Sacrifice to Aid Fertility

The sacrifice of the Pawnee girl and the eating of her heart described at the beginning of this chapter are representative

11. Seligmann, *Melanesians of British New Guinea*, p. 462.
12. E. Tregear, *Maori Race*, p. 360.
13. Thomas Williams, *Fiji and the Fijians* (London: Alexander Heylin, 1858), p. 206.
14. Meek, *Northern Tribes of Nigeria*, vol. 2, p. 60.

of a variety of instances of human sacrifice and cannibalism performed in the interest of aiding nature.

Sacrifice and the Scapegoat

In the Old Testament, we read of the ritual of the scapegoat, in which the sins of the community are symbolically laid upon a goat that is driven into the wilderness. The community is left morally purified. It is reasonable to suppose that in the original form of the rite the scapegoat was a scapeman and that his flesh was eaten.

> The victim was conducted to an Ebwo tree to which he was bound after his arms and legs had been tied; the king stepped forward and solemnly transferred first his own sins, then the sins of his household, and finally the sins of the community to the head of the sacrifice. The trespass-transfer being thus fulfilled, the man was loosed from the tree (his legs and arms remaining bound) and a rope was attached to his ankle and forthwith he was dragged round the town by two slaves appointed to the task. The whole populace treated the wretched creature as an accursed thing; he was reviled, spat upon, kicked, stoned; dust was thrown upon him, and in every form imaginable he was despitefully treated and denounced as an abomination. The slaves continued to drag him through the streets until life was extinct, and then the corpse was taken back to the king's quarters and cast away in the spot reserved for the bodies of human sacrifices. The victims were not buried; they would have been left to rot but for the fact that the corpses were stolen during the succeeding night by the friends of the official executioners who were not members of that community. The bodies were taken away to the native town of these officials and were there eaten.[15]

The next step in the development of this sacrificial ritual was to have a scapeman who was merely killed and his flesh left untouched. The Yoruba were a noncannibal people living in proximity to other peoples who practiced anthropophagy.

15. G. T. Basden, *Among the Ibos of Nigeria* (London: Seeley Service, 1921), p. 232.

They had a ritual of scapeman similar to the one quoted from Basden above but with the significant difference that the man's body was never eaten.[16]

Sacrifice to Insure Success in Warfare

The outward form of ritual sacrifice is a standard one, no matter what the particular object to be gained is. Water may be used in connection with making rain, or corn seed in making the crops fertile. The particular desire is incidental to the outward form of the rite: something is killed in order that benefits may accrue to the community. When the Yoruba sacrificed a victim to the war-staff, the warriors rushed in to drink a drop of his blood. Sometimes this was licked from the executioner's sword; with other tribes, only the executioner had the privilege of tasting the man's blood; in one tribe, a special attendant to the high priest was called *Osi* ("the blood licker").[17]

These examples demonstrate the close connection between sacrifice and cannibalism and between sacrifice and aggression. For the eight categories of benefits that accrue from sacrifice, one could undoubtedly find examples where human sacrifice is practiced but the flesh is not eaten. Similarly, one would find examples in the eight situations where animals are sacrificed and the flesh of these animals eaten. In agricultural societies, the fruit of the earth is "offered up" as a sacrifice. Finally, there is a stage of development and sublimation where prayers are offered up to prevent calamity, to avoid famine, to provide success in warfare, to take away our sins, and so on through the same list of deep human needs.

It seems clear that there is a definite developmental sequence in the ritual of sacrifice: (1) there are cannibal societies that have no notion of the idea of sacrifice; (2) human beings are sacrificed and the flesh devoured; (3) human beings are killed as an offering, but the corpse does not provide a meal; (4) animals are sacrificed and human beings

16. Talbot, *Southern Nigeria,* p. 858.
17. Ibid., p. 867.

are not. At each new stage, a substitution takes place. But it is no mere substitution; it is not a replacement of goats for sheep. This kind of substitution is the very basis of the sublimation of aggression. When people kill an animal instead of a man, they are not merely substituting one object for another. The animal symbolizes the man, just as killing the man symbolizes the cannibal act. With each increasing symbolization, mankind develops further from the actual psychological source of aggression. As the object of aggression becomes increasingly symbolized, the expression of aggression becomes increasingly sublimated; at the same time, the affectionate feelings inherent in all aggressive acts grow at the expense of aggressive desires. The affectionate quality of the act becomes more and more prominent and the aggressive qualities retreat to the background, so that today we see in the visual symbol of the crucifixion and in the communal act of the eucharist only affectionate qualities. We may be repelled, at first, to be told they contain within their forms expressions of the deepest, most primitive aggressive desires. And yet, it is precisely because they do contain and satisfy these desires in a sublimated way that they have succeeded in civilizing us.

In his description of Aztec ritual, Murdock closes with an apologia for the Aztec: "Even the cannibalistic sequel, far from being a gross orgy of savage gluttony, was to the Aztec a rare spiritual experience. In consuming the flesh of the human representative of his divinity, he was uniting himself with the divinity. What the devout Christian does when, in the sacrament of the Eucharist, he partakes figuratively of the body and the blood of his God, the Aztec still did in a strictly literal sense, inspired, moreover, by an identical emotion and conception."[18]

The Christian and the Aztec may be inspired by an identical emotion, but they are not inspired by an identical conception. It is precisely in the *conception* that they differ so radically. The Christian concept of divinity is far different from the Aztec concept; the quality of love inherent in Chris-

18. Murdock, *Our Primitive Contemporaries,* p. 396.

tian divinity is inconceivable for the Aztec. The Christian idea of the satisfaction of primitive aggressive needs is far removed from that of the Aztec. The cannibal activity of the Aztec is not a "rare spiritual experience"; it is a gross spiritual experience that is one of the least civilized aspects of Aztec society. It is true that the Aztec does literally what the Christian does symbolically, but it is precisely upon this capacity for symbolization and sublimation that culture is built and civilization erected. It is very important to point out the similarity of the psychological emotion in the Christian and the Aztec, but it is false to equate (psychologically and morally) a literal and a symbolic act.

Looked at more carefully, it appears that even the Aztec does not literally do what his emotion inspires him to do. He does not literally eat his god; he only eats a man who impersonates the god—who symbolizes him. He cannot literally eat the god because he does not exist; the god himself is a symbolic expression of an inner psychological state. The god who is eaten is a symbolic representation and projection of an ancient psychological desire.

The primitive psychological emotions that inspire the Aztec and the Christian are identical, but the *form* of these two religions differs radically: the form of Aztec sacrifice is hardly identical to that of Christian sacrifice. Form changes radically when there is a significant alteration in the balance of contradictory and ambivalent emotions. Affection and aggression are one such set of contradictory emotions. All sacrificial rites fulfill the desires for aggressive and affectionate satisfaction, but all forms do not do so in the same proportion. The amount of aggression in the Aztec sacrificial form is far greater than in the Christian, and the degree of affection far less. It is a mistake to say that between the two there is nothing to choose.

Freud states that a fully developed symptom contains within it both the negative, repressive elements that prohibit full satisfaction of an instinctual desire and a substitute satisfaction of that desire. We may regard symbolic form as a healthy version of a symptom; it can contain within it the satisfaction (albeit in a symbolic way) of a desire that has been given up, along with the satisfaction of the demands of conscience and the superego that call for abandoning that desire.

When a human being is sacrificed but his flesh is not eaten, the symbolic form of the sacrifice takes both these things into account. The form is constructed out of what *is* done and what *is not* done. A human being is killed: his life is destroyed; he is transformed from a living to a dead person. His flesh, however, is not eaten. The psychic drive institutionalized within the culture that says, "Thou shall not eat human flesh!" is revealed to have the power to prohibit the eating of the flesh. When an animal is sacrificed, the sacrificial rite includes the unconscious idea that a human being is *not* being sacrificed.

The blood of a sacrificial animal plays a crucial role in the rites of ancient Greece and ancient Israel; it does so because it is reminiscent of the blood of a human being. Human bodies do not resemble animal bodies, but if the blood of a sacrifice is poured upon the altar, it is difficult to know from the blood alone whether it is human or animal. When the sacrifice of human beings is no longer problematic for the culture—when the desire is so deep in the unconscious that it is no longer a viable temptation—at this point, the blood of the sacrificial animal ceases to be an important part in sacrificial rites. The blood of the sacrificed animal becomes the symbol of what is being done (an animal is being killed) and what is not being done (a human being is not being killed).

Through the mechanism of sublimation, the form provides a symbolic satisfaction for an aggressive desire that is not directly satisfied. The desire for cannibalistic experience is not satisfied directly in human sacrifice, the desire to kill another human being is not satisfied directly in the rite of animal sacrifice, and the desire to kill an animal and spill out its blood is not directly satisfied in the offering of first fruits. But in each case, a symbolic, sublimated satisfaction substitutes for direct gratification of the desire.

Moreover, only if a means is found to satisfy aggressive needs symbolically is it possible to give up aggressive practices. The more effective the rite is in remembering and symbolically satisfying these ancient aggressive desires, the more effective the rite will be in allowing us to give up the literal satisfaction. The pious Christian symbolically drinks the blood and eats the flesh of Christ because he does not eat the flesh of humans, nor kill them in a sacrificial rite, nor even does he destroy the body and life of an animal. It was Christianity that put an end to the most barbaric, aggressive performances in the Roman arena; it was Christianity that performed an act of symbolic cannibalism as a central rite of the religion. These two things are not contradictory; the performance of a ritual act of cannibalism is intimately connected with the capacity to give up literal acts of barbarism. For four hundred years, the Roman world had enjoyed the sport of watching animals consume human bodies and the spectacle of human beings destroying each other. In a remarkably short time. Christianity put an end to all of it.

The early Christian did more than this. He insisted that a slave had a soul; that a slave could go to heaven or hell; that Christ had died for the sins of slaves as well as of free men; and that a slave was, in fact, human. Recalling the history of the world up to that point, it was a remarkable statement. The fact that it took nearly two thousand years for mankind—and for Christians—to abolish slavery is proof of how slowly culture may change and develop. In spite of this, it is nonetheless remarkable that a religion could take such a stance at that time. The affectionate instinct that human beings feel for all other human beings received formidable aid. When symbolic form succeeds in effectively sublimating aggressive instincts, an increase in the open expression and satisfaction of human affection is the result.

The Psychological Origin 5 of Aggression

An understanding of the origin of aggression must begin with the idea of *instinct*, or preferably, *instinctual drive*. It is very difficult to define what an instinctual drive actually is. We can observe the manifestations of instincts in, for example, the development of a child, but that is not the same as defining what an instinct *is*. It will be sufficient for my purposes if we can furnish a description of how instincts operate—if we can understand the workings of instinctual drives within the psyche and in the world outside the psyche.

It is fair to call any psychic drive an instinctual drive if it meets two conditions. The drive should be universal for all humankind and it should not need to be taught; it should be there and manifest itself whether the child is instructed about its existence or not. A good example of such an instinctual drive is the Oedipus complex. It is not necessary to instruct a four- or five-year-old child that it is about to enter a phase of exhibiting intense sexual feelings toward the parent of the opposite sex and strong aggressive feelings toward the parent of the same sex. The psyche of the child arrives at this situation on its own, regardless of what the parents or the culture may or may not do. Any similar psychic drive that is independent of the actions of parents or culture may be described as instinctual.

This does not mean that the actions of parents and culture

have no effect on ways in which instinctual drives are manifest. Parents and culture may, and fortunately do, react to the child's instinctual drives in an enormous variety of ways. The culture and the parents may do their utmost to repress an instinctual drive, to sublimate it, to ignore it, to channel it into other directions, to heighten its manifestations, or to emphasize some aspects of the drive and repress others. There is no end to the catalogue of various responses, just as there is no end to the variety of human cultures that have been erected over a universal instinctual foundation. The fact that there are many different cultural systems is no denial of the existence of universal instinctual drives. Human history is the story of the multifarious cultural reaction to universal instinctual drives within the psyche.

It is reasonable to view the problem of human aggression and instinct from either of two points of view, which are not necessarily in opposition to each other. On the one hand, it can be maintained that aggression—the desire to fight, to kill, to injure, and to dominate other human beings—is a universal, instinctive drive in all people.

On the other hand, human aggression may be regarded as a reaction to frustration; when a person is thwarted in his or her desire for some object or condition, he or she will react with feelings of aggression toward those who are the cause of that frustration. One can imagine a different human psyche than the one we have; one can imagine human beings instinctively reacting to frustration with laughter or sadness or total lack of concern. Yet, this does not seem to be the case. Even if human beings do not have a primary instinctive drive toward aggression, nevertheless the universal human reaction to frustrated desires appears to be an aggressive one. Thus, aggression may be described as the universal instinctive reaction of human beings to frustration.

In either case, human aggression is inevitable: there can be no individual or social life without frustration; there can be no individual or social life without aggression. Considering the enormous role that institutionalized aggression has played in the history of the world, we may assume that we are dealing with a drive of enormous power.

In *Civilization and Its Discontents,* Freud addresses himself to the problems of aggression and its implications for the process of building and preserving civilization.

> In all that follows I adopt the standpoint, therefore, that the inclination to aggression is an original, self-subsisting instinctual disposition in man, and I return to my view that it constitutes the greatest impediment to civilization.[1]

Freud discusses not only the pervasive quality of aggression in our social life but also touches on the human reluctance to admit to its importance.

> The element of truth behind all this, which people are so ready to disavow, is that men are not gentle creatures who want to be loved, and who at most can defend themselves if they are attacked; they are, on the contrary, creatures among whose instinctual endowments is to be reckoned a powerful share of aggressiveness. As a result, their neighbour is for them not only a potential helper or sexual object, but also someone who tempts them to satisfy their aggressiveness on him, to exploit his capacity for work without compensation, to use him sexually without his consent, to seize his possessions, to humiliate him, to cause him pain, to torture and to kill him. *Homo homini lupus.* Who, in the face of all his experience of life and of history, will have the courage to dispute this assertion? As a rule this cruel aggressiveness waits for some provocation or puts itself at the service of some other purpose, whose goal might also have been reached by milder measures. In circumstances that are favourable to it, when the mental counter-forces which ordinarily inhibit it are out of action, it also manifests itself spontaneously and reveals man as a savage beast to whom consideration towards his own kind is something alien. Anyone who calls to mind the atrocities committed during the racial migrations or the invasions of the Huns, or by the people known as Mongols under Jenghiz Khan and Tamerlane, or at the capture of Jerusalem by the pious crusaders, or even, indeed, the horrors of the recent World War—anyone who calls these things to mind will have to bow humbly before the truth of this view.

1. Sigmund Freud, *Civilization and Its Discontents,* trans. James Strachey (New York: W. W. Norton, 1962), p. 69.

> The existence of this inclination to aggression, which we can detect in ourselves and justly assume to be present in others, is the factor which disturbs our relations with our neighbour and which forces civilization into such a high expenditure [of energy]. In consequence of this primarily mutual hostility of human beings, civilized society is perpetually threatened with disintegration. The interest of work in common would not hold it together; instinctual passions are stronger than reasonable interests. Civilization has to use its utmost efforts in order to set limits to man's aggressive instincts and to hold the manifestations of them in check by psychical reaction-formations.[2]

In this book about cannibalism, we have added many examples to Freud's historical list.

Freud's discussion of aggressive instinctual drives is confused in his use of the word *thanatos* for these drives. Most of the time, Freud uses the word *thanatos,* or "death wish," to describe a drive within the psyche towards self-destruction—and not to describe the wish for the death of someone else. When he sets eros against thanatos, it appears, at times, that he is saying that there are two diametrically opposed instinctual drives: one toward life and love and the other toward death and self-destruction. It is not clear whether thanatos also means destruction of the life of *others*.

Freud may mean that there are two *separate* instinctual drives: one of self-destruction and one of aggression; or, rather, he may mean that there are two aspects of a single aggressive-destructive instinctual drive—the drive towards aggression being a primary one and the self-destructive feelings merely secondary, when the aggressive drive is turned inward. "The fateful question for the human species seems to me to be whether and to what extent their cultural development will succeed in mastering the disturbance of communal life by the human instinct of aggression and self-destruction."[3] In this sentence, the implication is that aggression and self-destruction are two aspects of one human instinct.

In my view, this last formulation is the correct one. There

2. Ibid., pp. 58–59.
3. Ibid., p. 92.

is one instinctual aggressive-destructive drive; sometimes it is directed outward and is named *aggression,* and sometimes it is directed inward and is called *self-destruction.* The relationship between aggression outward and self-destruction inward is the same as that which Freud discusses under the headings of *sadism* and *masochism.*

Masochism results when an intense aggressive feeling is repressed and, therefore, turns inward and is directed at the ego itself instead of at an external object. A child having a tantrum is a good illustration of the phenomenon of aggression-destruction and sadism-masochism. The child is intensely angry because his wishes have been frustrated, usually by a parent. The aggressive feelings are incapable of fulfillment, so that the child begins to be destructive to *itself.* He kicks himself, he bangs his head on the floor, and he punishes the frustrating parent by punishing himself.

I have pointed out how rites of mourning for the dead often include self-destructive aspects: the mourner spills his own blood or cuts off a finger. In the sacrificial form, some sort of self-destruction is always evident; hence the name *sacrifice.* One always destroys something that is of value to oneself: a child, an animal, or a piece of one's own body. In that state of civilization where bloody sacrifice is a central rite, the sublimation of aggression is only partially accomplished, and much aggressive energy is simply repressed. When aggressive energy is repressed, as opposed to sublimated, it turns inward and becomes self-destructive. The ritual of sacrifice sublimates whatever aggressive energy may be sublimated and represses the rest, but it also manifests this repressed energy in a self-destructive way and even makes a virtue of the giving up—of the sacrifice. As civilization advances—as the sublimation of aggression does its job more and more completely—then the need for repression diminishes. It is no longer necessary to perform rites of bloody sacrifice.

There is a profound, ambiguous relationship between aggression outward and self-destruction. The first objects of aggression are the very same people who give love to the infant and the child and thereby make its life possible. The child identifies with its parents at all stages of development. When the child grows up, becomes an adult, and kills, he is always killing—unconsciously—someone who has been the object of love and someone with whom he has identified. From the recent war in Vietnam, we have the following edifying quote: "I ran that little mother all over the place hosing him with guns but somehow or other we just didn't hit him. Finally he turned on us and stood facing us with his rifle. We really busted his ass then. Blew him up like a toy balloon."[4] From this point of view, all satisfaction of aggression outward is an act of self-destruction. One cannot kill without, in some way, killing one's self. We have come very close to understanding the basic ambivalent situation in all aggressive behavior.

Freud's theory of the instinctual nature of libidinal drives and their development through various stages is much more generally known and accepted than his views on aggression. What is the relationship between the development of the libido, or of libidinal instinctual drives, and instinctual aggressive drives? Freud never addressed this question. There seems to be a *parallel* development between the libido and aggressive drives. Psychoanalysis identifies oral aggression: in the stage of oral libido, when aggression is concentrated in the mouth. For every subsequent stage of libidinal development, there seems to be a stage of aggressive concentration in the same part of the body. There are references in psychoanalytic literature to *anal sadism,* which obviously corresponds to the anal stage of libidinal development. The child moves on to a genital stage, which can provoke *genital aggression.* In the Oedipus complex, which is the subsequent libidinal state, half of the conflict is erotic and the other half is aggressive—the desire to eliminate the parent of the same sex.

Even the superego, the heir of the Oedipus complex, has its aggressive component and can become sadistic toward the ego.

4. Quoted by Philip Slater in *The Pursuit of Loneliness* (Boston: Beacon, 1970), pp. 38–39.

> This we can study in the history of the development of the individual. What happens to him to render his desire for aggression innocuous? Something very remarkable, which we should never have guessed and which is nevertheless quite obvious. His aggressiveness is introjected, internalized; it is, in point of fact, sent back to where it came from—that is, it is directed towards his own ego. There it is taken over by a portion of the ego, which sets itself over against the rest of the ego as super-ego, and which now, in the form of "conscience," is ready to put into action against the ego *the same harsh aggressiveness that the ego would have liked to satisfy upon other, extraneous individuals* [author's italics]. The tension between the harsh super-ego and the ego that is subjected to it, is called by us the sense of guilt, it expresses itself as a need for punishment.[5]

The obscenities of the street teach us that one can utter an aggressive outburst to correspond with any libidinal stage. The oral imprecation urges one to "go suck on a lemon!" The anal curse tells one to "go shit in your hat!" or threatens that one is going to "bust your ass!" The genital stage has a standard form, "Fuck you!" The satisfaction of Oedipal desires brings down the aggressive condemnation, "You motherfucker!" And even the superego can be an ally in the desire to destroy one's enemy, "God damn you!"

The tendency of aggression to attach itself to, and express itself in, libidinal terms supports the idea that aggressive instinctual drives are reactive to frustration and are not primary drives. If aggression is an instinctual reaction to frustration, and if a large part of all frustration is libidinal—as it must be—it is natural that aggression express itself within the particular libidinal state that is being frustrated. Oral aggression, then, in this view, is a reaction to oral frustration; the persistence throughout life of Oedipal aggression is a reaction to Oedipal frustration. From a logical standpoint, this point of view has much to recommend it. From a slightly different point of view, it can be argued that aggressive feelings are primary but they require an object onto which they can become attached—that they need a "local

5. Freud, *Civilization and Its Discontents*, p. 70.

habitation and a name."[6] Whether aggressive instinctual drives are primary or secondary (that is, reactive), they are obviously of enormous importance and exert an all-pervading influence on our private and social lives.

Freud also addresses himself to this issue, although he is not trying to solve the identical problem.

> In the most recent analytic literature a predilection is shown for the idea that any kind of frustration, any thwarted instinctual satisfaction, results, or may result, in a heightening of the sense of guilt. A great theoretical simplification will, I think, be achieved if we regard this as applying only to the aggressive instincts, and little will be found to contradict this assumption. For how are we to account, on dynamic and economic grounds, for an increase in the sense of guilt appearing in place of an unfulfilled *erotic* demand? This only seems possible in a round-about way—if we suppose, that is, *that the prevention of an erotic satisfaction calls up a piece of aggressiveness against the person who has interfered with the satisfaction,* [author's italics], and that this aggressiveness has itself to be suppressed in turn. But if this is so, it is after all only the aggressiveness which is transformed into a sense of guilt, by being suppressed and made over to the super-ego. I am convinced that many processes will admit of a simpler and clearer exposition if the findings of psycho-analysis with regard to the derivation of the sense of guilt are restricted to the aggressive instincts. . . .
>
> When an instinctual trend undergoes repression, its libidinal elements are turned into symptoms, and its aggressive components into a sense of guilt. Even if this proposition is only an average approximation of the truth, it is worthy of our interest.[7]

The reason that these statements are only approximations of the truth is that they refer to post-Oedipal situations and not to situations of a pre-Oedipal nature. The frustration of oral aggression cannot result in a sense of guilt because the sense of guilt is predicated on the existence of the superego, as Freud himself infers. There is no superego in pre-Oedipal

6. *A Midsummer Night's Dream,* act. 5, sc. 1, line 17.
7. Freud, *Civilization and Its Discontents,* pp. 85, 86.

situations, since the superego comes into existence as a result of the resolution of the Oedipus conflict. A strong sense of guilt or sin is lacking in almost all primitive societies. Kluckhohn remarks of the Navaho: "As a matter of fact, it may be questioned whether minimally acculturated Navahos ever feel 'guilt'—in the sense of anxiety or self-punishment for undetected acts which are, however, known to bring disapproval or punishment if observed by others. 'Shame' as opposed to 'guilt' is a striking Navaho configuration. 'Conscience' is hardly an important deterent of action for Navahos—only anticipation of actual overt punishment."[8]

Yet, people who live in primitive cultures do go through an Oedipal stage. However, primitive culture is characterized by a concentration on pre-Oedipal problems. Problems of oral aggression, a magical view of reality, and the emotion of shame are widely characteristic of all primitive cultures.[9]

The superego has very little to do with the origins of aggression. Whether aggressive drives are primary or a secondary reaction to frustration, the original object of these aggressive drives is the mother, or that female adult who is primarily responsible for the early nurturing of the child. In primitive cultures, the situation of close biological dependence of the child upon its mother is maintained much further into the child's life than is true in our society. The median age for weaning a child in fifty-two societies studied by Whiting and Child is two and a half years.[10] If aggressive instinctual drives are primary, they will certainly be directed in the beginning at the object that is most important in the child's life; if these drives are reactions to frustration, it is natural that they be directed at the person responsible for the frustration. In either case, the mother of the child is the first recipient of the child's aggressive feelings.

8. Quoted in John W. M. Whiting and Irvin L. Child, *Child Training and Personality* (New Haven and London: University Press, 1953), p. 230n.

9. The transition from "shame culture" to "guilt culture" in ancient Greece has been brilliantly documented by E. R. Dodds in *The Greeks and the Irrational* (Boston: Beacon Press, 1957).

10. Whiting and Child, *Child Training and Personality,* p. 70.

Oral aggression requires an oral object of that aggression. To contend that the primary object of aggression is the father is to expound the view that a child's aggressive feelings do not develop until the third or fourth year of its life. Such a view is untenable. "The dread of being *eaten* I have so far found only in men; it is referred to the father, but it is probably the result of the transformation of oral aggressive tendencies directed upon the mother. The person the child wants to devour is the mother who nourished him; in the case of the father there is no such obvious occasion for the wish."[11]

The mother plays two essential roles: she is the primary source, at the beginning, of all the biological and psychological satisfactions that the child needs for life; she is also, however, the first object of powerful feelings of aggression. It is no wonder that in adult life, the basic human attitude toward aggression is one of ambivalence. There used to be a popular song extolling the virtues of *mother,* which started by listing the virtue that begins with M, and then O, and so forth. "Put them all together, they spell *mother*" the last line concluded. One comedian sang a humorous version of the song that ended, "Put them all together they spell *mother;* don't bite the hand that's feeding you!"

If the primary objects of affection and the primary objects of aggression are identical, the situation of ambivalence creates a condition of conflict within the family. Not only is the expression of aggression filled with ambivalence because of the existence of intense feelings of affection for the objects of this aggression, but feelings of affection toward these objects are filled with ambivalence because of the multifarious feelings of aggression that adhere to the very same people. The human resolution of these conflicts consists in *the projection outward and away from the family of both the affectionate and aggressive drives.* "In young children, for

11. Freud, "Female Sexuality" (1931) in *Sexuality and the Psychology of Love,* ed. Philip Rieff (New York: Collier, 1963), p. 206.

instance, ambivalent emotional attitudes towards those who are nearest to them exist side by side for a long time, without either of them interfering with the expression of the other and opposite one. If eventually a conflict breaks out between the two, it is often settled by the child making a change of object and displacing one of the ambivalent emotions onto a substitute."[12] On the institutionalized social level, these conflicts are resolved by the displacement of these feelings—both affectionate and aggressive—outside the clan or outside the tribe or village.

Every known human society has some sort of incest taboo. Incest may be defined only in terms of the immediate family, but it may also include all the women or men of one's mother's or father's totem or all the women or men of one's own clan or tribe. Exogamy is the custom whereby ego must seek his or her marriage partner outside a particularly defined unit of clan, totem, tribe, or village. Even though one's primary sexual and affectionate drives take as their object the members of one's immediate family, one must seek the satisfaction of these impulses *outside the family* in order to become an adult. The same thing is true for aggression; there is a universal incest taboo and there is also a universal taboo against matricide, patricide, and fratricide.

One marries outside the area of incest taboo, and one kills outside the area of aggressive taboo:

> Your own mother,
> Your own sister,
> Your own pigs,
> Your own yams that you have piled up,
> You may not eat.
> Other people's mothers,
> Other people's sisters,
> Other people's pigs,
> Other people's yams that they have piled up,
> You may eat.[13]

12. Freud, *Group Psychology*, trans. James Strachey (London: Hogarth, 1959), p. 11 n. 1.

13. Margaret Mead, *Sex and Temperament in Three Primitive Societies* (New York: Mentor, 1950) p. 73.

The ambiguity in the poem reflects the truth behind these two taboos. Does the poet mean that you do not eat your own mother or your own sister, or does he mean that you do not sleep with your sister or mother? Being a poet, he means both. He is showing us the continuity of taboo, both sexual and aggressive, and he also shows that its function is to displace its two aspects outside the family. The main result of these outward displacements is that conflicts within the family are lessened, the stability of the family is assured, and new adults set out to establish new families of their own.

Society is the family writ large. It suffers from the same conflicts of aggression and affection within its ranks. It resolves these conflicts—at least partially—by displacing aggressive instinctual feelings outward, away from the tribe. "It is always possible to find together a considerable number of people in love, so long as there are other people left over to receive the manifestations of their aggressiveness."[14]

The Iroquois understood this principle extremely well:

> "Dreams are not to brood over, to analyze, and to prompt lonely and independent action; they are to be told, or at least hinted at and it is for other people to be active." The dreamer hints at the nature of his dream to the tribal leaders who then decide on the interpretation of the dream and on what is to be done to satisfy the wishes expressed in the dream. There were also customary rules about the manner in which certain types of dream wishes were to be satisfied. "Dreams in which hostility was directed at members of other nations were properly satisfied by acting them out both in pantomime and in real life; but bad dreams about members of the same community were acted out only in some symbolic form, which had a prophylactic effect."[15]

The cannibal does not kill members of his own family or clan in order to eat them, except in certain exceptional and explainable situations. The cannibal eats those who are *other* —who are *not me*. Civilized society enslaves or exploits or

14. Freud, *Civilization and Its Discontents*, p. 61.
15. Thomas H. Hay, "The Windigo Psychosis: Psychodynamic, Cultural and Social Factors in Aberrant Behavior," *American Anthropologist* 73, no. 1 (February 1971): 8–9.

makes war on those who are not me—those who are not human. The verbal transformation of a "yellow gook" into a "little mother" tells us an enormous amount about the origin of and the satisfaction of the human desire to kill.

If there were a perfectly nurtured child, he or she would still have aggressive drives. It is not the job of nurturing to eliminate all aggressive feelings from the child's psyche, even though the properly raised child will have much greater freedom in the expression of his or her affectionate feelings because aggressive drives will have been thoroughly sublimated. If a child is perfectly nurtured through the oral phase (this is not very likely to happen, but it is worth considering from a theoretical point of view), it still arrives at a state of Oedipal conflict; full development as an adult requires this. In this latter stage, strong feelings of aggression are manifest, unconsciously and consciously, against the parent of the same sex, who stands in the way of the satisfaction of libidinal desires. The aim of proper child-rearing is not to prevent this from happening but, rather, to respond in a manner that will help resolve the conflict and the ambivalence.

Aggression has its uses. The goal of proper education of a child is to prevent it from feeling guilt or shame about any instinctual feeling it has. If a feeling is inevitable, it is natural; the child should be taught that there are no unnatural natural feelings. He or she must be permitted expression of his or her aggressive feelings because if their release is forbidden, these drives undergo a process of repression—not of sublimation—and repressed instinctual feelings will seek satisfaction. When society offers the individual the opportunity to satisfy these repressed aggressive drives by displacing them onto oppressed peoples, the temptation to do so is too great to be resisted.

If, as has been postulated, aggression is an instinctual drive, and if instinctual drives have enormous power within the psyche, how is it possible that these drives are overcome? What power is there within the psyche that is potent enough to repress or sublimate these aggressive drives so that an affectionate life and a stable society are possible? I have discussed at great length the sublimation of aggression and how civilized life—indeed, all cultural life, whether civilized or primitive—is possible only with the aid of this process. There must be some instinctual drive in opposition to aggression and at least as powerful (if not slightly more powerful) that operates within the psyche. An instinctual drive of the magnitude of aggression could only be countered by a different instinctual drive or drives. These drives are identified in psychoanalytic thought by the names of *libido* or *love* or *eros*.

When Freud first discusses libido and its development through definite stages, the word has primarily a sexual meaning. Freud is intent on demonstrating that the child has a sexual life and that this sexual life develops in a definite pattern as the child matures. There is never any doubt on the part of Freud, or even of his critics, that sexual drives are instinctual. Today, if you ask the average person what he thinks human instincts are, he will quickly respond, "Hunger, sex, self-preservation." The early critics of Freud questioned only whether one could ascribe sexual feelings to a child. There was, and is, no serious question of the instinctual nature of sexual drives and of their potency.

As Freud's thought advances and as the intense struggle to establish the fact of the sexual life of children subsides, Freud begins to use the words love or eros in place of the more sexual term libido. In this expansion of the conception of its nature, the fact that libido is an instinctual drive is always maintained. When Freud's thought reaches the point where a love of mankind and a devotion to abstract ideas are also subsumed under the notion of libido, he asserts that the drive in people that reaches out to extend the feelings of love toward all humanity is an *instinctual drive—a part of basic libidinal development.*

> Libido is an expression taken from the theory of the emotions. We call by that name the energy, regarded as a quantitative magnitude (though not at present actually measurable), of those instincts which have to do with all that may be comprised under the word "love." The nucleus of what we mean by love naturally consists (and this is what is commonly called love, and what the poets sing of) in sexual love with sexual union as its aim. *But we do not separate from this—what in any case has a share in the name of love—on the one hand, self-love, and on the other, love for parents and children, friendship, and love for humanity in general, and also devotion to concrete objects and abstract ideas* [author's italics].[16]

It is true that in other places Freud postulates the idea that there is a conflict between erotic drives and civilization that is, by nature, repressive toward these drives. In these passages, Freud is using the word eros in a strictly sexual sense, not in the expanded meaning that has just been quoted. He is also trying to deal with the sexual repression of Victorian times—trying to explain this repression by a generalization to all forms of civilized society.

The real conflict—and Freud did not make this clear—is not between libido and civilization. The real conflict is between the purely sexual elements of libidinal drives and the more expanded, desexualized (sublimated) elements that we subsume under the word love. It is not possible for two mature adults to love each other without the sublimation of some of the purely sexual elements in the libido. The truth of this is pointed out when one observes that the purely sexual elements include a rather large dose of narcissism. Without the sublimation of narcissistic sexual libido, no mature love is possible—as so many have discovered, to their dismay. It is true that civilization has been built by means of the sublimation of primary sexual drives (including narcissism), but this sublimation has enabled other libidinal drives to be satisfied: friendship, love of humanity, and love of abstract ideas.

The drive toward civilization is an *instinctual drive*—a

16. Freud, *Group Psychology*, p. 22.

part of the relentless movement of the libido outward. "Civilization is a necessary course of development from the family to humanity as a whole. . . ."[17] It is not true that civilization is built upon the repression of the libido; exactly the opposite is true. Primitive society is maintained by repressing those instinctual libidinal drives that push the concept of love outward to include all mankind. It is primitive society that is the repressive one; in it, the concept of love is constrained and restricted by repression, its device used against eros and freedom. In the twentieth century too, repression is the mechanism used by the societies that refuse to extend the notions of freedom and love. Repression is the device used by cultures that wish to preserve within themselves the primitive notions of aggression that have survived into modern times.

Two fundamental instinctual drives exist within the psyche: affection and aggression. Both are of enormous power and of enormous importance, but they are in opposition to each other. Both are concentrated, in the early stages of life, on the same object or objects: first the mother alone and then both parents. It is dangerous for the psyche to repress either, since both are instinctive drives; hence, the great importance of the process of sublimation. Aggressive drives are sublimated so that libidinal drives may be fulfilled. There is no such thing as pure aggression because aggression always has an object and that object can never be pure, since we must always have a mixture of love and aggression toward it. We should not be surprised to find a large degree of affection hidden within aggressive behavior—we should be surprised if we did not find it.

We begin our study of the nature of aggression by trying to understand cannibalism, in the hope that it will help us understand all forms of socially institutionalized aggression. The cannibal is an adult living in a cultural system; both he and the system preserve and institutionalize attitudes appro-

17. Freud, *Civilization and Its Discontents*, p. 80.

priate to an infant in the oral stage of development. All adults and all cultural systems provide for the satisfaction of aggressive drives; what distinguishes the cannibal is that he does this in the most primitive—social and psychological—way possible. "Identification, in fact, is ambivalent from the very first; it can turn into an expression of tenderness as easily as into a wish for someone's removal. It behaves like a derivative of the first, *oral* phase of the organization of the libido, in which the object that we long for and prize is assimilated by eating and in that way is annihilated as such. The cannibal, as we know, has remained at this standpoint; he has a devouring affection for his enemies and only devours people of whom he is fond."[18] We understand the poet who tells us that we always kill the thing we love; it is much harder to see, but equally true, that we always love the thing we kill.

There is a profound difference between an individual psychic drive and a cultural system that incorporates that drive; for instance, there is a profound difference between oral aggression and cannibalism. The difference lies precisely in the nature of any cultural system. For an individual psychic drive to be incorporated into a cultural system, that drive must be institutionalized, and in the process of institutionalization, a transformation takes place. A cannibal is *not* an infant eating his mother; a cannibal is an adult living in a society—an adult capable of performing adult functions: marrying, having children of his own, and providing physically for his family and for the preservation of the culture in which he lives. Institutionalization of psychic attitudes, no matter how primitive, requires the establishment of cultural forms, which contain much more than the original psychic drives that give them the energy for their being. Among other things, cultural form is deeply involved with the existence of conscience, or superego, since all cultural forms are products of society as well as individual psychic drives. The oral aggression of an infant knows nothing of the superego, but the cultural form of cannibalism cannot exist without it.

18. Freud, *Group Psychology,* p. 37.

All cultural form has the capacity to deal, within the form, with ambivalent and contradictory drives. Seen from one point of view, this is precisely the task of the configuration. Cannibalism is not a pre-formal, pre-social entity. It is a social form that deals with the basic ambivalent nature of all aggression, and of oral aggression in particular. It does so, first, by directing aggression outward away from the tribe and the family and, second, by containing within it some aspect of that affection present in all aggression.

Karl Abraham observes the workings of ambivalent oral aggression in one of his patients:

> For our patient's behaviour fully coincided with that of an infant. . . . He said that when he was a little boy he had had the idea that loving someone was exactly the same as the idea of eating something good. Since childhood he had had "cannibalistic ideas." These ideas were at first traced back along associative paths to his fourth year. At this age—I was able to check the correctness of his statements as to the date—he had had a nurse to whom he had been very much attached. It was she who was the centre of his cannibalistic phantasies. At a later period the patient still often used to want to bite her, and "to swallow her, skin, hair, clothes, and all."[19]

A cultural form, to be successful, must in some way reconcile, in part, these opposing ambivalent views. The process of eating the dead, which I have labeled affectionate cannibalism, succeeded in doing just that. It is exciting to find that one of Abraham's patients recreated for himself that successful cultural form: "Abraham describes a depressed patient whom he was treating who lost his appetite and suffered further relapses following the death of his wife. One night, the patient dreamed, in thinly disguised fashion, of eating the body of his wife. Following this dream, the patient's appetite returned and his progress in analysis accelerated."[20]

All cultural forms work, they contain and reconcile (partly) ambivalent attitudes, and those that have to do with

19. Karl Abraham, *Selected Papers,* trans. Douglas Bryan and Alix Strachey (London: Leonard and Virginia Wooff, 1927), pp. 256–257.
20. Hay, "Windigo Psychosis," p. 4.

aggression contain elements of affection as well. But this does not mean that any form is as good as any other because they are both forms. Cannibalism is one such form, and Athenian democracy is another. As cultural forms develop, aggression is increasingly sublimated and libidinal feelings of love and conscience are enhanced. "If this is correct, we may assert truly that in the beginning conscience arises through the suppression of an aggressive impulse, and that it is subsequently reinforced by fresh suppressions of the same kind."[21] The more there is of aggression, the less there is of love and of conscience; the less there is of aggression, the more there is of love and of conscience. A time of radical moral change, such as we are living in today, is no time for "cultural relativism," because cultural relativism means moral relativism—and for a person of conscience, that is intolerable.

21. Freud, *Civilization and Its Discontents,* p. 77.

The Uses 6 of Aggression

Some aggressive acts serve useful and humane purposes. When aggressive drives are sublimated, and not repressed, aggressive energy is available to the psyche to do necessary work. A sublimated use of aggression is necessary for a child to mature and grow into an adult, and this sublimated use of aggression is also incorporated into cultural forms.

In addition to the ambivalence between aggression and affection, which we have looked at already, there is another basic ambivalence all people face: the polar desires of independence and dependence. Infants are born completely helpless, both physically and psychologically; they are dependent upon those around them for all their needs. At first, dependency is necessary for survival; infants must learn to trust the situation in order that they may obtain the physiological and psychological values they will need later.

As children mature, they gradually become more and more independent, which means that they learn to depend upon themselves for their physical and psychological needs. At first, the process of growth is biological, but, after a while, it becomes psychological as well. When the psychological process begins, children tend to express reluctance to establish their independence because they sense that becoming independent has a negative component: the necessity of giving up the pleasures of dependency. The psyche may become split, longing for two opposite things, and may be described accurately as being in a state of ambivalence.

We often hear about the bachelor who is psychologically dependent upon his mother and who has great difficulty in deciding to marry. He does not want to remain single, but he is reluctant to give up the pleasures of dependency—he is in a state of extreme ambivalence. If he meets a girl, falls in love, and inclines toward marriage, he still finds that he has an inner conflict. If he decides to resolve this conflict by taking the step toward independence, and if the conflict remains intense, there is one thing that he probably does. He becomes aggressive toward his mother: he exaggerates her faults; he projects onto her his own desires to stay dependent and accuses her of trying to keep him home and ruin his life; he indulges himself with outbursts of aggression directed at her. There is probably a scene between mother and bachelor, during which the latter tells her off and leaves, slamming the door. If this conflict were presented in a movie, the audience would applaud the moral use of aggression at this point. In *A Doll's House*, Ibsen's Nora finds that when all argument fails aggression is effective in a war of independence, and the slamming of the door (a sublimated aggressive act) becomes the symbol of her assertive independence.

A young couple I know had their first child, who was breast-fed by the mother. Contrary to the advice of the pediatrician and the wishes of the father, the mother insisted on nursing the baby beyond the recommended six months. After two months of this extended nursing, the baby took matters into its own hands or, more accurately, into its own mouth, proceeded to bite the breast and refused to nurse anymore. The significant thing for us is that the child did not just refuse to nurse, but it acted aggressively toward the breast before giving it up. The situation of dependency was broken with an act of aggression.

Slater describes a psychotic child who has a great desire to be enclosed in the "mother box" and yet has a great fear of being so contained. This dilemma is acted out by the child's enclosing himself in a box, or closet, or any dark place, and then bursting out, using his feet with aggressive abandon.[1]

In each one of these cases—the bachelor, Ibsen's Nora, the nursing child, and the psychotic boy—aggression against the object of dependency is used to free the subject from the confines of that dependency and bring a measure of independence.

When I was young, I assumed that all one needed to do to bring up a healthy child is to make sure that it is properly loved. Later, I found out that the really hard task is to give a child all the love it needs while educating it away from the situations of dependency toward independence. To smother with "love" the child's instinctual aggressive drives so that it is incapable of expressing aggression in the proper way is to cripple the child and leave it with no aggressive energy that can be used in the service of independence.

A child's instinctual aggressive drives cannot be allowed to run rampant, however; if this were allowed, the child would never mature emotionally and would always treat people as objects. On the other hand, situations of dependency must not be exaggerated, and the child must learn to become independent. This cannot be accomplished without the use of healthy aggressive instinctual drives. The giving of love is easy compared with the Scylla and Charybdis situation of dependence versus independence and expressing aggression versus sublimating aggression. Civilized cultures are much more indulgent of the expression of aggressive needs on the part of children than primitive cultures are; the latter are very repressive of aggressive manifestations in the young. Individual freedom—one of civilization's great gifts—is dependent upon the capacity of parents to allow children a healthy expression of their aggressive needs.

One of Freud's principal insights is in the realm of human needs beyond the simple ideas of pleasure and pain. There are those who argue that all human psychology can be understood as a desire to maximize pleasure and minimize pain; Freud, on the other hand, postulates in *Beyond the Pleasure*

1. Philip Slater, *The Glory of Hera* (Boston: Beacon, 1968), p. 93.

Principle that the psyche, as it matures, goes beyond the principle of mere pleasure and exhibits a desire for reality. He does not say that in reality there is no pleasure or that such desires for reality are masochistic because they involve the abandonment of pleasure. The conflict is not between reality and pleasure but between a desire for reality and *immediate* pleasures. The desire for independence is analogous to the desire for reality—neither can be achieved without the capacity to give up immediate pleasure. There is a great pleasure in reality and in independence, but a child has to be educated to these facts; he already knows the facts of immediate pleasure without instruction.

The attainment of reality and independence can be *temporarily painful.* A child must be educated to endure this temporary pain if it is to achieve the higher pleasures of reality and independence. These desires do not have to be taught; they are instinctual drives within the psyche. If they were not, they would never obtain the power to overcome entrenched, immediate satisfactions. The child's parents, and the culture in which they live, have the option of either encouraging or discouraging these drives toward independence. If they encourage the child, he or she is then in the position to use the available energy in the psyche to break the bonds of dependency and immediate pleasures.

Needless to say, the conflict of reality and pleasure principles will produce situations of ambivalence. Here again, aggressive energy is used by the ego to resolve the conflict, to add motive power to the drive to reality. The healthy child turns away with distaste, and usually with a verbal aggressive attack, from its most recent objects of dependency and pleasure. The child rejects the bottle, the blanket, the cuddly toys, and the childish stories that were told—all the symbols of past dependence and dependent pleasure. Without the aid of aggressive energy, the ego would be helpless against the temptation of past pleasures.

Keeping these ideas in mind, it is possible to make three general statements, which have been tested by others against certain social data.[2] First, when a child's physical and psychological dependency is preserved longer than is necessary, and when that individual in later life is expected to assume an aggressive adult role, then such a person will be forced to make use of violent aggressive acts that serve the purpose of breaking that dependency. Second, when the normal aggressive responses in a child are excessively repressed, it will seek violent and aggressive outlets for that aggression as an adult. Third, the first statement is not possible without the second—that is to say, it is impossible to keep a child in a prolonged state of dependency without repressing its normal aggressive responses.

The male child who is cared for in infancy and early childhood by a female—either his mother or a nurse—has a special problem. If he is kept in a prolonged situation of dependency on a female adult, and if his father is usually absent (for whatever reason), he identifies himself with females to an inordinate degree. This yields what is called "cross-sex identity."[3] For the male child, the father is critical in solving the problem of dependency. If the father is present and available to the male child, the child has the option of identifying with his father and breaking his infantile and childish dependency on the mother. If the male child is encouraged by his mother to be independent, his identification with his father develops earlier and more completely. The opposite mode, obviously, brings the opposite result.

2. I am indebted for these statements and throughout this chapter to the work of Beatrice and John Whiting and their associates (see works cited below). It is not accurate, however, to ascribe these propositions to the Whitings because the manner in which I have put them is not exactly the way the Whitings have stated them; in fact, I doubt whether the Whitings would agree with the way I put certain ideas. Without their work, however, my discussion of the relationship of child training to aggression in adult life would have been greatly diminished.

3. Beatrice Whiting, "Sex Identity Conflict and Physical Violence: A Comparative Study," *American Anthropologist* 67 (December 1965 Supplement): 123–140; R. V. Burton and J. W. M. Whiting, "The Absent Father and Cross-Sex Identity," *Merrill-Palmer Quarterly* 7 (1961): 85–95.

This brings us to the fourth observation: when the father is absent from the household most of the time, the male child becomes unusually dependent upon the mother (or nurse) and identifies with her to an excessive degree, so that when that child matures and wishes to assume an adult male role within society, he will be inclined to resort to violent, aggressive rituals and actions to break his situation of dependency and female identification.[4]

Primitive societies keep a child in a condition of psychological and biological dependency for a much longer period than do civilized societies. In *Child Training and Personality,* Whiting and Child report their cross-cultural study of child-rearing practices. Five aspects of human behavior are studied in over fifty societies: oral, anal, sexual, dependency, and aggression systems. Each of these particular systems is studied to determine whether a society is originally indulgent or severe in socializing the child to each particular system in the early years of the child's life. The same examination is made of the later years of the child's life. A society may be very permissive toward one system of behavior in the child's early years and yet extremely restrictive in the later years. The five systems of behavior in fifty societies are examined in terms of original indulgence and also for subsequent severity of socialization. Conditions in primitive cultures are checked against a study made by Davis and Havighurst of black and white middle- and lower-class families in Chicago in the early 1940s.[5]

"There are 52 societies for which we have our judge's estimates of the age at which serious efforts at weaning are typically begun. For the median case, weaning is reported to begin at the age of two and a half years. Approximately this age is indeed typical of primitive societies in general, for the estimate for 33 out of the 52 societies falls between the ages

4. J. W. M. Whiting et al., "The Function of Male Initiation Ceremonies at Puberty," *Readings in Social Psychology,* ed. E. E. Maccoby et al. (New York: Holt, 1958), pp. 359–370. Also Whiting, "Sex Identity and Physical Violence: A Comparative Study" and Burton, Whiting, "The Absent Father and Cross-Sex Identity."

5. J. W. M. Whiting and Irvin S. Child, *Child Training and Personality* (New Haven: Yale University Press, 1953).

of two years and three years." In the over-all rating of indulgence of oral desires, only one primitive society ranked lower than the Chicago middle-class groups; fifty-one out of fifty-two societies ranked higher in initial oral indulgence.[6]

This prolongation of the state of oral dependency results in an exaggeration of the weaning process, when the time comes to break this tie.

> When the Kwoma child is weaned, a number of drastic things happen all at once. He is suddenly moved from his mother's bed to one of his own. [The child, it must be remembered, is over two years old at this point.] His father resumes sexual relations with his mother. Although the couple wait until their children are asleep, the intercourse takes place in the same room. Thus, the child may truly become aware of his replacement. He is now told that he can no longer have his mother's milk because some supernatural being needs it. This is vividly communicated to him by his mother when she puts a slug on her breasts and daubs the blood-colored sap of the breadfruit tree over her nipples. Finally he is no longer permitted to sit on his mother's lap. She resumes her work and goes to the garden to weed or to the swamp to gather sago flour leaving him behind for the first time in his life. That these events are traumatic to the child is not surprising. He varies between sadness and anger, weeping and violent temper tantrums.[7]

That such a child may grow up with a desire to kill someone should not surprise us. And if his society provides him with legitimate satisfactions for this kill desire, it can be assumed that he pursues those satisfactions with great relish.

In South Africa:

> The very day of his weaning, the child must leave the village of his parents and go to stay with his grandparents. A little mat and a few clothes have been prepared for him and the grandmother comes to take him. . . . Sometimes father and mother accompany their offspring themselves, during the

6. Ibid., p. 70.

7. J. W. M. Whiting, R. Kluckhohn, and A. Anthony, "The Function of Male Initiation Ceremonies at Puberty," *Readings in Social Psychology,* p. 362.

> night, to make the separation easier. It is a sad day for them as well as for the child! The following day the parents go again to see how the little one has stood in their absence. They do not enter the village. They remain hidden in a little copse and look at their child through the branches! He must not see his mother, otherwise he would cry.[8]

Having suffered this humiliation, the child grows to become an adult and revenges itself on its parents—by doing the same thing to its own child. Thus it is that culture perpetuates itself.

In addition to the practice of extended breast-feeding, primitive cultures differ markedly from more advanced cultures in another area closely connected with dependency. In almost all primitive cultures, the baby sleeps with its mother during the whole of the nursing period. "Of over 100 societies on which we have data on sleeping arrangements, the American middle class is unique in putting the baby to sleep in a room of its own."[9] We can further appreciate the extent to which the situation of extended sleeping with the mother can produce an exaggerated dependency when we realize that in many cases the woman does not have intercourse with her husband all through this period; not only is the child deeply dependent upon its mother, but the mother is unusually dependent upon the child for emotional and sexual satisfaction.

When this dependent situation is combined with a society that places high value on assertive masculine behavior, Whiting and Burton have shown that the cultures usually have a violent, aggressive initiation ceremony for adolescent boys, the purpose of which is to break the over-dependency and over-identification with the mother. The situation of maximum conflict is one where a boy initially sleeps with his mother and where the family unit takes its residence with the husband's tribe, not with the wife's tribe. In this situation, the culture is controlled more fully by the men.

8. Henri A. Junod, *The Life of a South African Tribe*, vol. 1 (New Hyde Park, N.Y.: University Books, 1962), p. 60.

9. Burton and Whiting, "Absent Father and Cross-Sex Identity," p. 88.

> In our sample of 64 societies, there were 13 in which there were elaborate initiation ceremonies with genital operations. All 13 of these had the exclusive mother-infant sleeping arrangements which we predicted would cause a primary feminine identification. Furthermore, 12 of these 13 had patrilocal residence which we predicted would produce the maximum conflict in identity and hence the need for an institution to help resolve this conflict. A chi-square test of the association is fantastically beyond chance. Expressed simply, 87½% of the 64 societies fall in the cells predicted by our hypothesis.[10]

When the father is absent from the home for a great deal of time, the dependency of the child—either male or female—upon the mother is exaggerated. This may happen in our culture in families of sailors, salesmen, and some executives; it was also seen during World War II. Many urban families, especially in ghetto areas, are one-parent units where the father is completely absent. In all of these situations, there is a profound increase of aggression when the male child feels the need to break his dependency on his mother and assert his masculinity.

Studies of delinquent children show that there is a remarkable tendency for them to come from homes where the father is absent. We are not surprised to find that boys who come from homes of this sort resort to violent and aggressive actions during the critical adolescent period. In a study of the sons of sailors, it is found that such children engage much more in compensatory, overly aggressive behavior as compared with boys of father-present families. Likewise, a study of boys who were infants when their fathers were away during World War II shows that when the fathers were absent the boys behaved like girls in fantasy and overt behavior, especially in regard to demonstrating very little aggression. When the fathers returned, their overt behavior remained somewhat passive, but there was a marked increase in the amount of aggression in fantasy behavior.[11]

There are circumstances within many primitive societies

10. Ibid., p. 90.
11. Ibid., pp. 92, 93.

that encourage the father to be absent during the first two or three years of the child's life. Only 20 percent of the societies in Murdock's *World Ethnographic Sample* are designated as strictly monogamous.[12] Most polygamous societies are those where a man may have several wives; there are very few polygamous societies where a woman may have more than one husband. In the more prevalent situation, it is probable that fathers have much less contact with their children than they have in a monogamous society; this is especially true during infancy, when the child is being nursed and sleeps with its mother. Intercourse is forbidden, so that the father does not sleep with the nursing mother at all but, instead, sleeps with those wives who are not so engaged. In fact, the cumulative taboos on intercounse for various ceremonial reasons, or because of menstruation, or because of an extended postpartum taboo leads William Stephens to speculate that sexual intercourse between a husband and a particular wife, in primitive cultures, is socially legitimate less than half the time.[13] In many primitive cultures, the father eats all his meals away from his family.

These three circumstances—extended breast-feeding, extended sleeping with the mother, the father's absence—all yield children overly dependent upon their mothers. When a male child who has grown up in such a situation of dependency is called upon by the process of biological growth and by his culture, to assume a masculine, adult role, such a child is much more inclined to resort to violent rituals. These rituals may be socially legitimate, and take place in violent initiation ceremonies, or they may be illegitimate, as with delinquent children in our society. Beyond adolescence, the adult male who is still unconsciously dependent upon infantile and childhood supports but who carries with him an ideal of masculine, independent behavior, will continue in the need to prove his masculinity and his independence of feminine support. He will eat people, he will kill people, he

12. W. N. Stephens, *The Family in Cross-Cultural Perspective* (New York: Holt, 1963), p. 33.
13. Ibid., pp. 10–11.

will make war, he will enslave others, and he will dominate and degrade women. He will do all these things under the banner of being a true man—of being strong and not weak. His real fear of dependency on feminine support remains hidden from consciousness.

Culturally speaking, it is men and not women who make war, enslave peoples, and domineer over others. A man revenges himself on his mother and asserts his independence of her (he feels) by going out to kill or eat someone and by domineering over his wife. His wife, in turn, revenges herself on him and on her own mother by seducing her children and causing them to be overly dependent upon her. The male children, in turn, grow up and revenge themselves on her by acting toward the world in the same way their fathers did. It is a pattern of behavior, created and reinforced by both psychology and culture, that becomes almost impossible to break and change.

If we leave aside the problem of delinquent children and look only at our overly dependent bachelor and at ritualized aggression within society, we must observe that from one point of view this aggression works. The bachelor does get married; the adolescent boys in primitive cultures do—after their violent initiation ceremonies—become adult men, living an adult life. These situations of over-dependency are broken; the bachelor and the adolescent boys proceed to live more independent lives than they were living before. The sorrow is that so much violence is necessary in order for them to become independent and that because of this the adult lives they do live are impoverished as a result of all the experiences necessary to become adult.

One crucial fact revealed by the cross-cultural study of child-rearing patterns is that primitive and civilized cultures treat expressions of aggression in the small child very differently. As we stated previously, Whiting and Child rank their five systems of behavior (dependence, aggression, oral, anal, and sexual) according to the degree to which they are indulged or repressed in the early years of the child's life. In primitive cultures, as one would expect, the dependency system ranks first as the most indulged in early childhood, and the oral ranks second. Aggression in the small child is the least indulged of the five systems; therefore, it is the most repressed of all.

In the American middle-class group, dependence is also the most indulged in the initial stages of the child's life, as it is in primitive cultures. Aggression, however, is the second most-indulged system of behavior, initially. The anal system is the least indulged of all. This striking fact is confirmed in a study made by Ryerson and discussed by Slater. Ryerson studied the medical advice given by doctors to mothers about child-rearing practices, particularly in England. From 1550 to 1750, this advice, if followed, results in child-rearing practices close to the median of the data Whiting and Child ascertain for primitive cultures. From 1750 to 1900, there is a marked decrease in the indulgence of four of Whiting and Child's five systems. Weaning comes earlier, toilet training comes earlier, the child is encouraged to sleep in its own room, the child's crying is to be ignored, it is to be handled less, and masturbation and sex play are more severely punished. The one exception to this decreasing pattern of permissiveness and initial indulgence is aggression—there is no marked increase in the repression of expressing aggression. While the other four systems are more strictly dealt with, the treatment of aggression remains the same and thus moves from fifth ranking in primitive cultures to second ranking in the American middle-class control group.[14]

This relationship between aggression and the other systems lends confirmation to my third hypothesis: excessive dependency can result only from the repression of the child's natural aggressive-independent drives. Primitive cultures repress natural aggressive and independence drives of the child, which process produces three results: (1) the child is excessively dependent upon parental care; (2) the transition to adult life and adult life itself are marked by the necessity to experience excessive violence; (3) the need for aggressive satisfaction in adult life is projected outward, away from the

14. Whiting and Child, *Child Training and Personality,* p. 114; Philip Slater, "Culture, Sexuality and Narcissism: A Cross-Cultural Study" (unpublished manuscript).

family and the tribe (which is really an extended family), in order that a reasonable amount of love can be expressed, making family and society possible. Primitive people do live more or less in harmony within their own families and within their own tribes. Love is possible (to a certain extent), and so is culture (to the same limited extent), because the powerful aggressive needs are satisfied exogamously.

Civilized cultures allow the child much more latitude than primitive cultures in the expression of its aggressive impulses. This occurs because the civilized parent is less ambivalent than the primitive parent in his feelings toward his own children. In primitive cultures, in spite of the fact that aggression is directed outward, the parent still retains a large reservoir of aggression toward its own offspring. The parent, therefore, reacts to any aggressive manifestation on the part of the child in a exaggerated way, making more of it than it really is. A civilized parent can deal with statements from a child, such as "I hate you!", with equanimity because the parent recognizes that the child does not mean exactly what it says. This equanimity and recognition are possible because the parent is sure of its own feelings of love toward the child; whatever aggression the parent may unconsciously feel it is able to handle.

Conservative, frightened members of our society believe we have raised a permissive generation that burns banks and bombs school laboratories. And Dr. Spock is the villain of the piece. It seems to me that we have raised a generation the finest members of which have as their ideals the final destruction of racism, the end to all aggressive wars, and a profound change in the gross materialism and absurd competitiveness of our culture. Their willingness to give up and sublimate these gross manifestations of aggression in adult life is related to the fact that their parents, sure of their own feelings of love, have permitted them the expression of aggressive feelings in infancy and childhood. It may very well be that Dr. Spock has had as much to do with it as his detractors think.

Sacrifice is a system of religious ritual that holds a crucial place in the religions of the world from primitive times to the most developed Christianity. Human beings feel the necessity to sacrifice when they are involved in a situation of *assertive action:* starting a journey, plowing a new field, building a new temple, eating the first fruits, starting a new year, going to war, getting married, or starting adult life. These situations of assertive action are deeply involved in the basic human ambivalence between dependence and independence. All assertive acts are independent; to do any of them, it is necessary to give up certain attitudes of dependence. This involves a conflict of ambivalent desires. The ritual of sacrifice resolves this conflict by doing two specific things: it satisfies the desire to stay dependent by rendering to the desire something that is precious, and it marshals aggressive energy against those psychic ties of dependency—it strikes back at them—so that the person who is asserting his independent drives is free to satisfy them.

All drives toward independent action are inhibited by fear of giving up the security of the dependent situation and fear of anticipated retribution from those (the gods, the parents) who do not want one to go. This second feeling—that they do not want one to do it—is itself the the result of two distinct feelings. First, the fear of leaving the dependent situation is projected onto others, so that the person involved feels he cannot leave because "they" won't let him. The bachelor is actually afraid to leave his mother and get married; this fear he projects onto her, thereby exaggerating, in his mind, her desires to keep him unmarried. The second part of this feeling that "they" do not want me to go is the fact that in many cases "they" *do not* want it. The bachelor is not necessarily just projecting; indeed, his mother may not want him to get married. The soon-to-be-initiated adolescent boy in a primitive tribe is not just projecting. He is fearful of becoming an adult; moreover, his mother may not want him to grow up. In many initiation ceremonies, the men of the tribe have to forcibly take the initiates away from their mothers, who weep copious tears when the boys are gone.

In the oral stage of development—and all sacrifice relates, in part, to that stage—the mechanisms of projection outward of inner feelings and of internal incorporation of outside reality easily pass into each other. The infant does not yet clearly distinguish between his own ego and the world about him. All internal fears are projected outward onto other objects; all external means of satisfaction and security are incorporated internally. If the child finds that the external world is partially hostile, as well as loving, it incorporates that hostility into itself, just as it projects outward its own inner hostile feelings. It is a time when there is no sharp distinction between self and objects.

> In this dependence on the mother we have the germ of later paranoia in women. For it appears that this germ is the surprising, yet regular, dread of being killed (? devoured) by the mother. It would seem plausible to conjecture that this anxiety corresponds to the hostility which the child develops toward her mother because of the manifold restrictions imposed by the latter in the process of training and psychical care, and that the immaturity of the child's psychical organization favours the mechanism of projection.[15]

When we talk of the institution of sacrifice, we must keep in mind that we are talking about adults engaged in adult activities. The ambivalence about independence, however, is a reflection of a much earlier stage of development. The degree to which the ego's own fear is projected onto others also determines the degree of violence necessary to break the tie that that fear represents.

A man wishes to set out on a dangerous voyage but he has all the ambivalence about it that we have discussed. What does he do? He sacrifices something; he kills something, and he goes. He sacrifices something—he gives up something precious to himself—in order to satisfy the thing in himself that says, "Do not go!" Pubescence is the beginning of the journey of adult life. In many primitive cultures, violent initiation ceremonies, marked especially by circumcision, are a required ritual for pubescent boys. The foreskin of the young boy is sacrificed. To whom? To the "gods" who cry, "Stay home! Don't go!" "The foreskins are dried and turned

15. Freud, "Female Sexuality," *Sexuality and the Psychology of Love*, ed. Philip Rieff (New York: Collier, 1962), p. 196.

over to the woman who has charge of the girls' initiation society, and they are cooked and eaten by all the girls. . . . In some tribes, after a boy has been circumcised, the blood from the wound is collected in a shield and taken to his mother, who drinks some of it, and gives food to a man who brought it to her."[16]

Not all sacrifice is to the mother; human development is more complex than that, and adults do not live their lives (even imaginatively) in the oral stage. Sacrifice is not to be understood, however, unless we can see its origins in very early psychic states.

Further, not all sacrifice is as sado-masochistic as the circumcision ritual, and even here, it is a ritual forced on the boys by the men. The man intent on his dangerous journey is more likely to kill a sheep or a goat or another man than he is to injure himself. If he be the leader of Greeks, he may even sacrifice his own daughter. His daughter is indeed his own, but the life he destroys is not his own; he continues to live. The killing of something in the rite of sacrifice is an act of aggression against that which says, "Don't go!" Aggression is used as an instrument of the assertion of independence—it is a wasteful, destructive instrument, but using it is better than staying home, if these are the only alternatives available. The particular instance of the sacrifice of one's own child is profoundly ambiguous, as the stories of Iphigenia and of Isaac demonstrate. It is the work of civilization to make more than two alternatives available; there is the third possibility available to those who are raised with love and freedom—to leave without sacrificing anything. Only a mature handling of the problem of human aggression makes it possible to reach this point.

The third thing our traveler does is to leave. We wish him fair journey.

16. Bruno Bettelheim, *Symbolic Wounds* (New York: Collier, 1962), p. 94.

Religion and Aggression:

7

The Sacred and the Secular

It is almost imperative to begin a discussion of religion and aggression with Durkheim. To understand the role of aggression within society, it is necessary to understand the role of religion within society and, then, the role of aggression within religion.

Two definitions of Durkheim's are central to this understanding:

> All known religious beliefs, whether simple or complex, present one common characteristic: they presuppose a classification of all things, real and ideal, of which men think, into two classes or opposed groups, generally designated by two distinct terms which are translated well enough by the words *profane* and *sacred* (*profane, sacré*). This division of the world into two domains, the one containing all that is sacred, the other all that is profane, is the distinctive trait of religious thought. . . .
>
> A religion is a unified system of beliefs and practices relative to sacred things, that is to say, things set apart and forbidden—beliefs and practices which unite into one single moral community called a church, all those who adhere to them.[1]

One may use the words *profane* and *secular* interchangeably, even though, traditionally, there is a usage that con-

1. Émile Durkheim, *The Elementary Form of the Religious Life*, trans. J. W. Swain (Glencoe, Ill.: Free Press), pp. 37, 47.

trasts *profane* with *sacred* and *secular* with *religious*. But it is important to distinguish between *religious* and *sacred*, since these terms have often been confused with each other. The two concepts of sacred and religious have been confounded, in part, because each of them seems to be opposite to the secular or the profane. But many things can be sacred without being religious, although everything that is religious is also sacred. The sacred encompasses an area larger than the religious—there are sacred things outside the sphere of religion. Thus, the two words are not interchangeable; we cannot say, "The sacred is a system of belief relative to religious things." Religion deals with sacred things; sacred things do not deal with religion. In fact, there are some sacred things that are not religious. A thing (an attitude, a feeling) may be sacred and not religious when it does *not* "unite into one single moral community. . . ."

The crucial quality that distinguishes the religious from the sacred arises from the concept of the *social*. Religious experience is social experience; it unites the believers into one single moral community. There is no religion without the social; sacred thought or feeling, if it is personal and private, is not religious.

Certain areas of human psychological existence always belong in the area of the sacred. At times, they may also be religious; at other times, they may have nothing of religion about them. Experiences involving death, magic, and fear are never profane or secular; they are always sacred, but they may be very personal and private—and therefore, not religious. It is difficult to define *the sacred;* yet we know that it deals with the irrational, the uncanny, and the unknown—the deep inner psychological forces—whereas the profane deals with common, ordinary, everyday rational and reasonable experience.

One realm of experience that is never common, ordinary, rational, and reasonable is the sexual. All sexual experience, for adults and for children, has something deeply magical and irrational about it. Sex is always sacred; whether it is religious or not depends upon the attitude of the particular society. We are, at present, engaged in a struggle to make sexual acts between consenting adults a private, personal matter about which society, as society, does not judge. We are attempting to define sexual acts between consenting adults as nonreligious acts. Insofar as society prevents abortion, punishes homosexuality, forbids the dissemination of birth control advice, and so on, to that extent society is insisting that sexual attitudes stay in the area of religion; it is insisting that all must "unite in one single moral community" in regard to sex. Taking sexual activity out of the area of the religious does not, however, make it profane. It remains sacred (charged with irrational energy), but it is privately, personally sacred.

Magic—the attempt to use supernatural forces in the realization of human desires—is another area of human feeling and reaction that is never profane or secular but may or may not fall under the heading of the religious. All religion has something magical in it; every church practices some form of magic. This does not mean, however, that all magical action takes place under church auspices. Magic within the church is religion; magic without the church is superstition. That the religion of one generation is looked upon by the next as superstition is a phenomenon with which we are all familiar. Playing the numbers, betting on horses, stepping on the cracks of the sidewalk, and playing the stock market—all this is magic outside the church, outside of religion. It is not rational, it is not common, ordinary experience, and it is not profane; it is a sacred but not a religious experience.

Fears of all kinds—the death of someone one loves, the knowledge that one is destined to die oneself—are areas of sacred action and reaction. Here again, these feelings are sometimes subsumed under religious experience—they are the concern of the whole community—and sometimes they are private. Further, an act may be either sacred or secular depending upon the conditions under which it is executed. Driving a car is an ordinary, everyday, secular act. Let an accident, or a serious near-accident happen, however, and the act of driving has brought one close to injury and death. Driving the car is no longer an ordinary, profane act. It may take many days or weeks before one drives again with an uncharged, rational attitude. Religion has nothing to do with it; the question is purely one of sacred or profane.

The feeling and expression of aggression, for an adult, is never a profane emotion or act. It is always charged with irrationality and magic. It may or may not be religious, depending upon the extent to which the community is involved. For example, two men have an argument in a bar and begin to pummel each other. No one is severely hurt, no legal charges are brought, and no officer of the law observes the action. It is an act of aggression, an irrational, sacred act, but it is not religious. On the other hand, the most powerful democratic country in the world decides that it will impose its will on a small, seemingly defenseless country in Southeast Asia. All the trappings of the corrupt superego (saving the world from the communist menace) are brought in to give the act the clothing of morality. It is a sacred act of aggression, full of irrationality, but it is also an act of religion because it involves the moral beliefs of the community.

In New Guinea, a stranger is found lost in the bush. He is captured, killed, roasted, and eaten without any ritual activity surrounding the act. Such an action is not religious because it does not involve the community in any moral activity. It is religious only in a negative sense—the religion does not forbid the eating of human flesh. Our "religion" not only does not command the eating of human flesh, it absolutely prohibits it; it does not allow for personal choice in this matter. The personal cannibalism that exists in some primitive cultures is still a sacred act, charged with irrationality and magic. I do not believe that anyone can eat human flesh knowing it to be such with the same everyday casualness with which one eats animal flesh. The magical, charged situation inherent in cannibalism can never be secularized no matter what the circumstances are.

In Africa in the area of the Congo, human flesh was once sold in the marketplace for home consumption. The tribesmen along the Lulongo River organized raids on the upper reaches of their river, overpowering the people, killing some in the process, and taking captives away with them. When they had accumulated a sufficient cargo of these human cattle, they set out with them to the Mobunji river, where they sold the captives for ivory. The purchasers proceeded to feed the starvelings until they were fat enough for the market, butchered them, and sold the meat in small joints. Sometimes a section of a town bought a large piece of the body wholesale and then retailed it out. A head of a family might purchase a whole leg and then divide it between his wives, his children, and his slaves. There is similar evidence from the Pacific of the retailing of human flesh. "But reluctantly I must confess that where, as in San Cristoval, after a battle we find dead bodies hawked up and down the coast in canoes for sale, we come very near the cannibalism of our boys' story-books." In these circumstances, there is as little of religion as there is in playing the horses. Neither, however, is a profane act.[2]

It is fascinating to discover that the vocabulary of some cannibals makes a distinction between human flesh consumed under religious auspices and flesh that is eaten casually or privately. "Such feasts as I saw then, or what I saw of them, were bona fide *Kawpi purai.* By that I mean that human flesh eaten was that of enemies killed in a fight; but I have been persuaded in my own mind, over and over again, that the desire in some of the old men for human flesh was so rampant that they killed their own people and ate them when they could not kill their enemies to appease their cravings. Surreptitious cannibalism, however, does not come under the head *Kawpi purai.* It was not a feast to them, but a mere meal."[3] The distinction is clear; the feast, *Kawpi purai,* is a religious act—it unites the people into one single moral community after killing enemies. Private, personal cannibalism was not *Kawpi purai;* it was a private act for private pleasure.

2. Reverend W. Holman Bentley, *Pioneering on the Congo* (London: Religious Tract Society, 1900), pp. 211–212; Florence Coombe, *Islands of Enchantment: Many-Sided Melanesia* (London: Macmillan & Co., 1911), p. 221.

3. J. H. Holmes, *In Primitive New Guinea* (New York: Putnam, 1924), p. 173.

Among the Melanesians, Seligmann reports that a victim killed and eaten out of religious revenge was termed *maiha.* Anyone who was killed in a fortuitous way—and such people were killed only when no revenge was to be expected—was termed *idaïdaga.* An *idaïdaga* might be obtained from a shipwreck, or it could have been someone who had lost his way in the bush. In this particular case, even the eating of the *idaïdaga* was surrounded by rules and restrictions; there was actually very little ceremonial difference in the eating of the *idaïdaga* and the *maiha.* It is in the use of different terms that we see that one form of victim had a greater religious significance.[4] The distinction between religious and sacred is not always as sharp as that between a socially institutionalized act of magic and the private betting on horses. In the case of the Melanesians, one has to say, the eating of the *maiha* is more religious than the eating of the *idaïdaga.* The latter is also religious, but it has some element of the nonreligious sacred in it. If it did not, there would be no reason to have two different terms for the same act.

The Role of Aggression within Religion and Culture

It is a crucial function of all religions in all cultures to distinguish between legitimate institutionalized social aggression and illegitimate aggression. In a cannibal society, cannibalism is a legitimate form of social aggression; the legitimation of that aggression is a religious act.

In a noncannibal society, cannibalism is an illegitimate form of aggression; religion says so. The certification of legitimate aggression is a universal and crucial area of religious action, but it is not religion's only sphere. In a democratic society, politics assumes the role of religion because politics is a discussion of what should be the "beliefs and practices which unite into one single moral community." This debate involves deciding what acts should be considered legitimate institutionalized aggression.

4. Seligmann, *Melanesians of British New Guinea,* pp. 548–559.

In a head-hunting, noncannibal society, head-hunting is a legitimate form of aggression; cannibalism is an illegitimate form. In a society that practices human sacrifice but forbids both cannibalism and head-hunting, human sacrifice is a legitimate form of aggression; the other two forms are not; the distinctions between the three are religious ones. Europeans of the twelfth century, the time of the Crusades, allowed the grossest form of aggressive behavior (barring cannibalism) against "the infidel"; on the way to Jerusalem, some of the Crusaders engaged in the first pogroms against Jews in European history. Such behavior toward Christians was considered intolerable. A fierce discussion ranged through western Christendom at that time whether this murdering of Jews was a legitimate act.

All societies, thus far, have practiced some form of aggression against human beings; social aggression, in certain specific forms, has been sanctified and legitimated by the religion of every society. In fact, the pursuit of aggressive satisfaction under the banner of the superego is one of the characteristics of any religious system. But the definition of what is legitimate aggression is subject to change, which can only come about through radical upheaval in the religion of the society. A new religion, or a new phase of an old religion, is capable of declaring illegitimate a form of social aggression previously tolerated or encouraged. Thus it was that Islam prohibited female infanticide and Christianity put an end to the barbarism of the arena.

It is a critical time for any society when it is engaged in such a redefinition of legitimate aggression. Such changes are usually accompanied by great conflict, unrest, and a heightening of the level of violence and civil strife within the culture. The United States has witnessed three such critical times in its history. The first was during the Revolution, a struggle against imperialism without and Tories at home who did not want independence and were suspicious of the democratic inclinations of its leaders. The second time was centered in the Civil War, when slavery was made illegitimate as a form of institutionalized social aggression. The third crisis is going on today. Two forms of legitimate aggression are under attack: racism at home and imperialism abroad. Racism (the domination of one race by another) and imperialism (a stronger country imposing its will on a weaker society) are indeed forms of aggression. The real conflict in America today is whether they are to remain legitimate or whether we, as a society, can further sublimate aggression, declare these forms illegitimate, and thereby increase the amount of eros in our cultural life.

That cannibalism is a form of institutionalized aggression is easy to see—the victims are killed and eaten. Other forms of institutionalized aggression are not as easy to recognize, particularly when domination has replaced killing. The desire to kill and eat has been sublimated into the desire to dominate and oppress. Any form of domination and oppression is an act of aggression on the part of the oppressors. Cannibalism, aggressive warfare, and conquest have been replaced, in the internal affairs of civilized society, by subtler forms of domination: slavery, racism, religious oppression, and capitalism.

The domination of women as a class by men as a class functions differently. Men never set out to kill and eat or conquer women as a whole class of people; they always dominate and tyrannize over women in a subtler way. Nevertheless, it is a tyranny—an act of institutionalized aggression. This, too, is under critical attack in our culture today, and this attack is part of the revolutionary change in moral values that is now possible within our culture.

With the sanction of religion—which unites into one single moral community—all cultures have permitted some forms of aggression and forbidden others. In response to aggression, eros has used the words of the Deuteronomist, "Thou shall not!" You shall not offer human sacrifice, but you may destroy, totally, the city of Jericho. You shall not watch wild beasts destroy human beings in the arena, but you may kill every Moslem you find in the conquered city of Jerusalem. You shall not own slaves, but you may tyrannize and brutalize all those in society who were once slaves. You shall not engage in constant feudal warfare, but you may send eight-year-old children into factories to work twelve hours a day and you may assault the leaders of the workers who come to organize your factory. You shall not destroy the countries of Germany and Japan, even though they have made the most aggressive of wars against you, but you may tyrannize Asians and blacks and Latin Americans because they are not powerful, industrial peoples—that is, they are not yet to be considered fully human. You shall not beat your wife, nor divorce her without compensation, but you may continue to domineer over her in a thousand subtle and not-so-subtle ways. *Culture* makes these statements; *religion* within culture sanctions these partly moral, partly immoral attitudes toward reality. It is the development of culture and religion that forces the increasing sublimation of aggression and, thereby, the increasing satisfaction of eros. These partly immoral values cannot be institutionalized within a culture without the repression of eros, and this repressed eros represents a vast reservoir of potential for change and development in any culture.

The fact that all cultural forms have permitted some kinds of institutionalized aggression does not mean that all cultural forms are more or less alike. Looked at superficially, the amount of aggression seems to be the same in all societies, but it is the quality, not the amount, of aggression that is most important. The direct aggression of the Aztec and of the cannibal is of a different quality from the more sublimated aggression of the Christian and the capitalist. The more aggression is sublimated, the more eros is expressed and satisfied. The very thing that makes us give up cannibalism, head-hunting, human sacrifice. the pleasures of the arena, and human slavery will allow us, and command us, to give up racism, war, and the domination of women by men. Eros is the driving force of cultural development, and the human capacity for sublimation and the creation of forms are the means by which its mission is accomplished. In this day of atomic warfare and revolutionary change, only eros will rescue us—let us not make the mistake of thinking we can be saved by anything else.

The Search for Elementary Form

The social "sciences" have not yet succeeded in doing what the physical sciences have done—that is, they have not clearly identified elementary forms. Durkheim thought that if we should succeed in finding an elementary form of religious life, it would make possible a more accurate understanding of all forms of religious life; all later, more developed forms of religious life would incorporate these elementary forms in a transformed way. Although he devoted a book to the search for this elementary form, he did not quite find it.

Anthropologists made great contributions to the understanding of religious life by revealing certain primitive religious attitudes that could never be seen by studying advanced forms. Ideas such as *mana, taboo,* and primitive sacrifice were revealed by the studies of primitive cultures, and it quickly became apparent that these notions were useful in analyzing advanced, developed, complex religions. Primitive notions of religion were still to be discerned in the historical religions, although in a transformed state. The studies of the religion of the Old Testament and of ancient Greece took an entirely new turn when people became aware that the explanation of what was really going on in the religions of Jerusalem and Athens lay in primitive religion. One could not really comprehend the prophet Isaiah or the deep religious aspects of Greek tragedy without understanding the nature of *taboo, mana,* and primitive sacrifice, among other things.

One reason for the power and permanent relevance of Freud's thought is the fact that he succeeds in identifying an elementary form of psychic life. A child at its mother's breast is doing something partly *sexual;* Freud calls it a manifestation of *libido.* When two adults are engaged in sexual intercourse, they are also manifesting libidinal energy; there must then be some connection between a child at its mother's breast and the sexual intercourse of two adults. In fact, the oral libido of the nursing infant is an elementary form of sexual life. No full understanding of developed, complex forms of adult sexual life is possible without an understanding of this elementary form of libido, and of all the changes, transformations, repressions, and sublimations that it goes through as the human organism develops. In essence, we cannot understand what two human adults are actually doing when they engage in sexual intercourse unless we understand what the infant is doing at its mother's breast. Freud not only hypothesizes the libido as the elementary form of sexual life but traces its history from infancy to adulthood.

Cannibalism is the elementary form of institutionalized aggression. It is not the elementary expression of aggression, since such an expression is a psychological, not a social, entity. Cannibalism is a cultural and social form; it is not merely a psychic attitude. The institutionalization of oral aggression is a crucial part of the cultural form of cannibalism. In order for a psychic attitude to become institutionalized, cultural form must incorporate it; that cultural form, however, contains much more than just a psychic attitude of aggression. It is also necessarily concerned with society and morals—in short, with religion: that which unites into one single moral community.

Religion requires conscience and a superego. Even the cannibal has them; they are stunted in their growth, but they do make unconscious negative judgments on the performance of cannibal acts. A purely psychic feeling, as opposed to its institutionalized form, may be unambivalently aggressive. Yet, the institutionalization of aggression within cultural form cannot be one dimensional; form is too complex for that. All cultural forms contain elements of eros as well as elements of aggression. Thus it is that any institutionalized attitude of aggression within cultural form must be ambivalent—form holds these two contradictory impulses together in one place.

If, as I have postulated, cannibalism is the elementary form of institutionalized aggression, then all subsequent forms of social aggression are related to cannibalism in some way. There is something of cannibalism in all subsequent, sublimated forms of institutionalized aggression. I do not mean to postulate an identity between an elementary form and developed forms: two adults having sexual intercourse are not doing what an infant does at the mother's breast, but there is something of oral libido incorporated and sublimated in the adult sexual act. Likewise, an adult who practices and votes racism is not a cannibal, but there is something of cannibalism incorporated and sublimated in his actions.

In the history of the sublimation of social aggression, killing and eating give way to just killing; killing itself gives way to dominance and tyranny; dominance and tyranny are further sublimated into competition—a form of aggression that takes its satisfaction from winning because there is always someone who loses. When this winning and losing refer to sporting activities, it may be innocent enough; but when it becomes an institutionalized social form and the losers are left to live in intolerable conditions, without adequate food, clothing, housing, medical care, education, or expectation of life, then such a system of winners and losers (competition) is an institutionalized form of aggression. It is a tyranny, although less obvious than an openly expressed tyranny. It is a hypocritical tyranny, but we must treasure and expose that hypocrisy because within it we will find the possibilities of further change.

War, slavery, racism, imperial domination, destruction of infidels, fascism, the tyranny of men over women, and capitalism are all the descendants of cannibalism. Insofar as the children are an improvement on their parents, we honor them, but we should not make the mistake of previous generations and assume that we have achieved the very highest pinnacle of civilization that people can attain. The struggle for the complete liberation of eros is an unending one.

Sublimation

8

The history of the Kwakiutl is an instructive case study of the transformations—the sublimations—that aggressive instinctual drives have undergone. Before the advent of Europeans and Americans, the society was extremely aggressive and competitive, engaging in restricted cannibalism, avid headhunting, and frequent warfare. When the more primitive expressions of aggression were limited by contact with civilized men and by the internal development of the culture itself, the Kwakiutl developed a unique cultural form—the *potlatch*—one of the most aggressive competitive "games" invented by any culture.

The data on this transformation are complete and unambiguous. All these forms of aggression (cannibalism, headhunting, warfare, slavery, potlatching) are intimately connected with each other; there is an easy flow of human energy from one form to the other. The Kwakiutl themselves were consciously aware that potlatching was a substitute for more aggressive forms. In many instances, the sublimation of aggression was not complete, so that the competitive experience of the potlatch very easily degenerated into a more primitive expression of aggression. We can observe the same phenomenon in our culture today when the spectators at a sporting match (which is a highly sublimated aggressive experience) end up quarreling and physically assaulting one another.

The purpose of the potlatch is to defeat one's enemy by

showing that one can give away or destroy more valuable property than he can. No attempt is made to hide the intensely competitive nature of the experience. As strange as this kind of activity may sound to us, we can observe a highly sublimated form of the same idea in our own society. The public giving away of money by philanthropists can also assume a highly competitive air. In such cases, especially when the giving away is done at a pledge dinner, rivalry and competition play a crucial role. The participants are giving away a part of their wealth in order to show how much wealth they actually possess. The pleasure of demolishing one's rivals by giving away the most is not absent from these occasions.

During intervals of time when there was no formal potlatch activity, the Kwakiutl satisfied their aggressive feelings toward others by destroying some of their own wealth. A *copper* was a decorated piece of copper of very high value. It was the most valuable single piece of property in the culture and was worth hundreds of blankets.

> And he threw the copper on the ground saying, "You, Wilson, we have also heard that you are another one who don't want our nephew to change his position, and here is another copper for you, and I am giving it to you to make you shut up." They put these two coppers together and he says to the young men to take these out to the deep water there and drown them. That means that they want to drown old Whanuk and Charlie Wilson. . . .
>
> "That was why I warned you not to come near my house and wake the baby up, but since you have wakened him up, today I am going to break this big copper for you two that have been making the noise." And he cut half the top off and another corner from the bottom and gave one part to each of the Mamaleleqala chiefs that threw their coppers into the water. Then he says: "Hap-hap-hap! I've eaten you. You are all in my belly now."[1]

As mentioned earlier, the cry *"Hāp-hāp-hāp!"* was the cry of the cannibal who was a member of the cannibal

1. Clellan S. Ford in *Indians of the North Pacific Coast,* ed. Tom McFeat (Seattle: University of Washington Press, 1966), pp. 131–133.

society. In both of these instances, a man felt that he had been wronged by someone else and sought revenge to even the score. In more primitive times, the offended man might have killed and eaten the offender, or merely killed him, or he might have engaged in sorcery to make him sicken and die. Here he did none of these things, but still his revenge had to be fulfilled. He satisfied his aggression in the sublimated way that was characteristic of the culture—he destroyed a valuable piece of his own property in the presence of the man who had wronged him. The fact that the Kwakiutl still preserved a restricted form of cannibalism (in the cannibal society) made it easy for him to express his revenge satisfaction in metaphorical cannibal terms.

The ceremony of the cannibal society itself was modified and sublimated during the time observers were recording their way of life. In the old days, the *hā'mats'a* (the cannibal) actually bit a piece of flesh out of the arm of one of his enemies. Subsequently, he merely pulled the skin up with his teeth and secretly cut off a small piece of it. He did not swallow this skin but hid it behind his ear, eventually returning it to its owner, in order to assure the latter that no witchcraft would be used against him by means of the skin.[2]

The restriction of cannibalism to certain members of society was, in itself, a mechanism of sublimation. In certain cultures, only the priests were allowed to eat the flesh. Among the Kwakiutl, only the members of the cannibal society engaged in anthropophagy; the majority of the culture did not eat human flesh. The society, as a whole, obviously enjoyed the vicarious cannibal experience of observing the *hā'mats'a*, but for them it was still a vicarious, not an immediate, experience. Looked at from one point of view, the Kwakiutl was "hypocritical" about his cannibalism. If the alternative, however, was for the whole society to do the real thing (kill and eat), then that hypocrisy had the value of being a sublimated experience that at least contained the possibility of leading to further sublimated forms.

Ritual sacrifice is a complex form that includes a good

2. Franz Boas, *Social Organization and the Secret Societies of the Kwakiutl Indians*, pp. 440–441.

measure of aggressive satisfaction. It has been observed that sacrifice is called into use on great occasions—occasions that call for an unusual expenditure of assertive energy. On such occasions, the Kwakiutl might destroy valuable property as a form of sacrifice, since this was the characteristic mode of sublimating aggressive impulses within the society.

> Property may not only be destroyed for the purpose of damaging the prestige of the rival, but also for the sole purpose of gaining distinction. This is done mainly at the time when houses are built, when totem poles are erected, or when a son has been initiated by the spirit presiding over the secret society of his clan. . . . It seems that in olden times slaves were sometimes killed and buried under the house posts or under totem poles. Later on, instead of being killed, they were given away as presents. Whenever this was done, the inverted figure of a man, or an inverted head, was placed on the pole. In other cases, coppers were buried under the posts, or given away. This custom still continues, and in all such cases coppers are shown on the post, often in such a way that they are being held or bitten by the totem animals. At the time of the initiation of a member of the clan slaves were also killed or coppers were destroyed. . . . The property thus destroyed is called the ō'mayu, the price paid for the house, the post, or for the initiation.[3]

This last is a wonderful illustration of the workings of the process of sublimation. The slave is no longer killed—he is given away instead—but the more primitive expression of aggression is remembered and symbolically preserved: the inverted figure of a man is placed on the poles. When one gives away the slave, one is imaginatively killing him; the figure of the man on the poles serves to make that imaginative killing more available to the mind. One may place a copper upon the poles instead of a man, and this is a further degree of sublimation, but even here the copper may be seen as eaten by the totem animal in order to remind us that in the imagination the totem animal is really eating the man. The cannibal past may be recalled simultaneously with the act of

3. Ibid., pp. 356–357.

sublimating aggression into much less primitive forms of satisfaction.

The exciting thing about the Kwakiutl is that they themselves were completely aware that the potlatch was a sublimated form of warfare.

> "Fighting with property" instead of "with weapons," "wars of property" instead of "wars of blood," are Kwakiutl phrases expressing what has proved to be a fundamental historical change in Kwakiutl life occurring within the period known to history. . . . The general conclusion is that the binding force in Kwakiutl history was their limitless pursuit of a kind of social prestige which required continual proving to be established or maintained against rivals, and that the main shift in Kwakiutl history was from a time when success in warfare and head-hunting was significant to the time when nothing counted but successful potlatching. . . .
>
> "We are of Ya'xsta L's blood. But instead of fighting our enemies with his death bringer we fight with these blankets and other kinds of property.
>
> "We are the Kaskimo, who have never been vanquished by any tribe, neither in wars of blood nor in wars of property. . . . of olden times the Kwakiutl ill treated my forefathers and fought them so that the blood ran over the ground. Now we fight with button blankets and other kinds of property, smiling at each other. Oh, how good is the new time!
>
> "We used to fight with bows and arrows, with spears and guns. We robbed each other's blood. But now we fight with this here (pointing at the copper which he was holding in his hand), and if we have no coppers, we fight with canoes and blankets.
>
> "True is your word. . . . when I was young I have seen streams of blood shed in war. But since that time the white man came and stopped up that stream of blood with wealth. Now we are fighting with our wealth.
>
> "The time of fighting has passed. The fool dancer represents the warriors but we do not fight now with weapons: we fight with property."

It would be difficult to exaggerate the degree to which the talk, the songs and the ceremonies of potlatching borrowed the metaphor of war and even developed it to the point where

> the metaphorical war had more meaning and thoroughness than their one time "fighting with weapons." The usual word for potlatch was "p! Esa," to flatten, and it came to mean to flatten a rival under a pile of blankets or "means of flattening," for the word for "potlatch blanket" took its origin from the same root and this literal meaning. The names of coppers often indicated that they were indeed the weapons of the new kind of warfare, potlatching: "War," "About whose possession all are quarrelling," "Cause of Fear," "Means of Strife." A great copper belonging to a chief was spoken of as his acropolis or fort on which he and his tribes could stand in safety and greatness. A broken copper was spoken of by its owners as "lying dead in the water off our beach" meaning that the breaking of it was as successful an attack against the rival as a killing would have been.[4]

The sublimation of aggression among the Kwakiutl was never entirely successful. Sometimes the competition of the potlatch resulted in more primitive expressions of aggression. In part, this was because the sublimation itself was caused by outside pressure from colonizers and not entirely from inner transformation. When recourse to aggression is relinquished thus, not from internal transformation, but because of external power, the result is not true sublimation but repression of aggressive satisfaction. When aggressive drives are repressed, not sublimated, the aggressive feelings are never really satisfied, and they never cease to demand satisfaction. They continue to exist in a repressed, unconscious state. In such a condition, they may reappear anytime and demand satisfaction.

The difference between sublimation and repression is illustrated by the famous story of Fast Runner and Throw Away, who conducted a memorable potlatch against each other. When the outcome of the competition was still in doubt, Fast Runner's two daughters volunteered to be thrown upon the fire. Two slaves were substituted for the girls, who went into hiding for four days, whereupon they reappeared from the ashes of the slaves. Throw Away was completely demolished

4. Helen Codere in McFeat, *Indians of the North Pacific Coast,* pp. 92–94, 95.

by this display of Fast Runner's privilege, and he had no alternative but to go away and fight the Nootka. Only one man returned to tell of the disaster of the war party.[5]

The Sublimation of Sexual and Magical Drives

The term sublimation is ordinarily used in a sexual context. I use this term in discussing human aggressive instincts because I feel that there are great similarities in the psychic processes involved in the sublimation of sexual and aggressive drives. In both areas of sublimation, the fundamental effect is the same. Sexual energy that is sublimated does not cease to be sexual; it continues as sexual in a more developed form. When aggressive drives are sublimated, they also continue as something aggressive; these sublimated drives obtain aggressive satisfaction, but in a more civilized way.

Both in cases of sexual and aggressive satisfaction, there is a profound difference between repression and sublimation. Sexual and aggressive instincts may be prevented from expressing themselves by external force; this force may come (in either case) from the culture, from parents, from an internal neurosis, or from an inadequately internalized superego. When sexual or aggressive instincts are repressed, and not sublimated, the desires themselves are not satisfied; they remain unsatisfied in an untransformed state—they are locked in a closet. The desires continue to exist in the unconscious and exert force toward satisfaction, thus forming an ever-present threat that they may come out of the closet and demand satisfaction. Sublimation allows for the symbolic satisfaction of these drives. True sublimation accomplishes the transformation of the drives so that they are no longer what they were; if sublimation has done its work, there is no threat that these drives will disrupt the orderly processes of life.

Sublimation is both a personal and a social process. The two aspects are not identical, but there is a very important

5. Ruth Benedict, *Patterns of Culture* (Boston: Houghton Mifflin, 1934), p. 199.

correspondence between them. New cultural forms have been created that provide for the increasing sublimation of aggressive and sexual instincts, but in order for these forms to last and do their work, there must be a positive acceptance of them by adults within the culture; they, in turn, teach the new cultural norms to their children. The original impulse for change within the culture comes from individuals who are, in turn, the products of as well as the makers of their culture. There is a constant interplay between the role of cultural form and the role of individuals in relation to that form. One thing is certain; if individuals do not have within them a strong desire for increasing sublimation, cultural form will never change.

Many who argue about the role of erotic freedom or restriction in the formation of civilized society confuse repression and sublimation. When sexual and aggressive desires are repressed, the individual ends up with less of a full human life; when, however, these desires are sublimated, the individual and the culture end up with more of a full human life. There are those who argue that society is opposed to erotic freedom and that this tyranny should be ended. Insofar as culture is repressive of sexual freedom—and it is—the assumption and the conclusion are correct; such repression should be eliminated. The culture also provides modes of sexual sublimation, however, and these modes of sublimation should be perfected, not done away with. Reading the exponents of "complete sexual freedom," one gets the feeling that he is being told to abandon all cultural mechanisms of sexual control, both repressive and sublimative.

Love is the greatest gift of sexual sublimation. Without the sublimation of sexual energies, there would be no mature love between adults; we would live only with lust, like the beasts of the field. Sexual energy itself is not one-dimensional; it begins in the mouth and travels to the anal regions before it finally focuses in the genitals. Without the sublimation of these earlier sexual forms, true genital sexual experience would be impossible. The most mature sexual experience that humans are capable of—the genital mating of two adults who love each other—does not take place without kissing, which is a mutual satisfaction of oral sexual energies. These oral desires are satisfied in a sublimated way; they are satisfied, but they lead onward to a deeper form of sexual satisfaction.

When one considers the possibility of complete sexual freedom, it is important to remember that narcissistic sexual satisfactions play an important role in all psychic life. Complete freedom rendered to narcissistic impulses results in an egocentricity that makes real love impossible. Mature love between two adults requires that each recognize the independent reality of the other; narcissistic experience is opposed to this recognition. Unlike Puritan society, our culture does not attempt to deal with narcissistic pleasures (such as dancing, bright colors, the theater, and so on) by repressing them. The satisfactory sublimation of narcissistic sexual energies is the precondition of real sexual freedom.

Men, especially in more recent times, have been repressive of the sexual drives in women. Victorian society set itself as an ideal the notion that women—but not men—should not experience sexual feelings and sexual pleasure. Gradually, our culture has lifted this repressive tyranny. In the struggle to put an end to sexual repression, some have made the mistake of wishing to destroy all forms of sublimation as well.

Freud postulated a period of sexual latency between the end of the Oedipus complex and the beginning of puberty as a fact of human psychic development. Malinowski found, however, that the Trobrianders had no period of sexual latency—that children eight and nine years old carried on sexually to the best of their abilities, with the joking approval of their parents and the culture as a whole. Malinowski's observations forced us to realize that the period of sexual latency is *culturally determined;* it is not an inevitable condition of the human psyche. Many primitive peoples had a much freer sexual life from puberty to marriage than exists in our culture. There were a handful of societies, like the Trobrianders, that had no restrictions on pre-pubescent sexual experimentation. The vast majority of human cultures, however, both primitive and civilized, saw fit to enforce a period of sexual quiescence between the end of the Oedipal stage and the beginning of puberty.

In the case of a culturally determined period of sexual latency in pre-pubescent years, the culture is clearly trying to encourage the development of factors in the psyche other than the sexual. It is a period of enforced sexual sublimation; sexual energies are restricted so that other ego qualities may grow. The restriction of sexual activity in adolescent children, which Western society has until most recently insisted upon, is not a process of sublimation, but one of repression. All restriction of sexual activity is not repressive, however; some is sublimative. The puritan sees all restriction of such activity as sublimative, although much of it is repressive. On the other hand, the advocate of total sexual freedom sees all restriction as repressive, although much of it is sublimative. When a sexual, or aggressive, impulse is forcibly restricted, this restriction may result either in a sublimated or repressive psychic experience. Barring any general rule that all restriction is good or bad, each impulse must be judged within its own particular circumstance. One may believe that children must be free to express aggression without concluding that any older sibling may be permitted to beat a newborn baby with a heavy instrument. Analogously, we may believe that children should not be sexually repressed without concluding that they should be allowed to masturbate in social circumstances.

Whether such a society is advisable or not, one can imagine a society where there are no sexual restrictions, either sublimative or repressive; one cannot do the same for aggression. A society where there are no restrictions of the expression of aggression would cease to be a society; it requires both the repression and the sublimation of aggressive instincts in order to survive. The degree of freedom in any society is dependent upon the degree to which aggressive drives are dealt with by sublimative, not repressive, means.

I cannot exhaustively describe the relationship between sexual and aggressive instinctual drives, nor the relationship between sexual and aggressive repression and sublimation; it is reasonable to say, however, that there is a definite significant relationship. I feel that only when we understand this particular relationship will it be possible to know how much the building of civilization depends upon the sublimation and repression of sexual drives. It is clear that the sublimation, and restriction, of aggressive instincts is crucial to the existence of civilized society. Yet, the question of the relationship of sexual drives to this process of sublimating and restricting aggressive drives is one that I cannot answer.

In addition to sexual and aggressive sublimation, there is a third area of human sublimation that plays a crucial role in the development of cultural form, and that is the sublimation of magic or, more precisely, of the magical attitude toward reality. The study of primitive culture and primitive religion demonstrates that the predominant attitude toward reality of primitive peoples is a magical one. Magical views of reality are not changed into something else as culture develops away from the primitive. When these attitudes are sublimated, they do not cease to be magical anymore than sublimated aggressive or sexual feelings cease to be aggressive or sexual. They continue as magical in a less primitive form.

Magic is sublimated into religion and into art. In the distinction Frazer draws, magic attempts to coerce reality into doing what the individual desires; religion, on the other hand, seeks the aid of a higher power, through prayer and supplication, to obtain its ends. Magic demands; religion supplicates. This distinction illuminates the characteristic quality in the magical attitude: magic believes that the world can be forced to do what the individual wishes to be done. Magic assumes that what I want and what exists are the same, and that if this is not so, the latter can be made to correspond with the former. Religion postulates a world out there that is not-me and does not correspond to my magical wishes. It is also based on the assumption that the world may successfully resist being coerced into corresponding to my wishes. Religion, as opposed to magic, postulates the existence of a moral world distinct from myself. Effective living in the world will, therefore, entail a change in me, an obligation to change myself in order to live in the real world. Magic asks for no change in myself except the acquisition of enough magical power to force the world to submit to my desires.

Although we can distinguish magic from religion in theory, in reality it is impossible to separate the two: there is no religion without magic. The degree to which magic is present in the total religious system is the degree to which that religious system is primitive. But religion does not make the magical attitude go away; religion develops by sublimating the magical attitude into something that is no longer purely magical but still retains something of the magical attitude; that something is religion itself. The degree to which magic is sublimated is the degree to which religion is civilized and has moved beyond the primitive.

As religion develops, it becomes increasingly concerned with morality. Increasingly, power resides in the moral stance, not in the magical. It is more magical and more primitive to kill one's enemy by sticking pins into his effigy than to call upon Yahweh to destroy him, but there is still something of the magical in asking Yahweh to do it. However, Yahweh may not listen. One may be unrighteous, lacking the right to call upon Him to do such a thing; one may have to change oneself—atone for one's sins—before Yahweh will perform this magical function. The sublimation of magic into religion leaves us with more, not less. We have more emotive life; we have more superego: we have Yahweh.

The difference between repression and sublimation in sexual and aggressive instincts also exists in magic and religion. The Sicilian peasants who in the nineteenth century threw images of saints into the creek in order to put an end to a drought were not regressing to a more primitive state from the lofty one of developed Christianity; they had never achieved this lofty state in the first place. The sublimation of their magical attitudes was very incomplete. Repression, not sublimation, prevented them from using primitive magical devices to end the drought earlier in the season; they were afraid of the priest. With these people, primitive magical attitudes had been repressed, not sublimated, by the power of the church.

Art is the other great form that is built by the sublimation of magic. The great pleasure in the experience of art is that of freely expressing one's magical desires in a controlled, sublimated way, under the guidance of the superego. Coleridge's "willing suspension of disbelief" is a great pleasure; humanity cannot live without expressing its magical desires. We may, however, prefer Shakespeare and Yeats to the shaman and the medicine man. Shakespeare and Yeats could not live without the shaman within themselves; in fact, Shakespeare's last great play has as its very theme the sublimation of magic.

> . . . I have bedimm'd
> The noontide sun, called forth the mutinous
>   winds.
> And twixt the green sea and the azur'd vault
> Set roaring war; to the dread rattling thunder
> Have I given fire and rifted Jove's stout oak
> With his own bolt; the strong-bas'd promon-
>   tory
> Have I made shake and by the spurs pluck'd up
> The pine and cedar; graves at my command
> Have wak'd their sleepers, op'd, and let 'em
>   forth
> By my so potent art. But this rough magic
> I here abjure; and when I have requir'd
> Some heavenly music (which even now I do)
> To work mine end upon their senses that
> This airy charm is for, I'll break my staff,
> Bury it certain fathoms in the earth,
> And deeper than did ever plummet sound
> I'll drown my book.[6]

The liberated person in the twentieth century who lives a good, examined life without god does so not because science destroyed religion and killed god. The sublimation of magic in religion had reached the point where further sublimation meant the destruction of the religious form itself. Science, unable to sublimate magic, does not satisfy the human craving for magical experience; it can never substitute for reli-

6. *The Tempest,* act 5, sc. 1, lines 41–57.

gion. It is art that has taken its place. Religion was destroyed and god was killed, not through the advance of science, but through the development of art and the relationship of self-conscious human beings to it. In art, as in all sublimation, we are left, not with less, but with more; the world is more real than it has ever been, and we are more real in the perception of it.

Human beings cannot live without satisfying their sexual desires and their aggressive desires, or without magic. But they may satisfy sexual cravings in love for spouse and children, they may slake aggressive desires in a humane politics, and art can fill their need for magic. It is a consummation devoutly to be wished! Without sublimation, it is all impossible—without cultural form that incorporates these sublimations, we would all be eating our enemies.

The Mechanisms of Sublimation

The mechanisms of sublimation are imaginative satisfaction, substitution, and restriction. The psychological purpose and accomplishment of all three of these devices is the replacement of symbolic for actual satisfaction. It is not necessary to directly satisfy an instinctual drive if one can manage to do it imaginatively. To look at it from the other side, it is only people who are incapable of doing certain things imaginatively who are forced to do them literally.

An illustration of this is provided by the resolution of the Oedipus complex. Freud asserts that the Oedipus complex comes to an end, and one of the singificant results is that a superego is now lodged in the child. His explanations of how this happens are not satisfactory. His most consistently held view is that a fear of castration causes the demise of the Oedipus complex. In other words, the situation is terminated because the child (male, in this particular discussion) cannot accomplish the goals set for him: to kill his father and capture his mother sexually. To see it in this way is to lay emphasis on the actual and not on the imaginative. Could one not say that the Oedipus complex comes to an end because the child accomplishes his goals; he kills the father and takes over the mother, but he does it imaginatively? In his imagination, he becomes the father; he has incorporated him and now stands in his place. It is for this reason that the child has a superego; the father has been internalized. The child, having taken the place of the father, now has everything the father had. The mother is only one of these things, for the father also has the power to make moral statements and to give moral commands. The person who used to say, "Do this," or "Don't do that," is now inside the child. It speaks with a voice that comes from inside: a still, small voice.

Near the end of his life, Freud postulated a view that related this incorporation of the conscience to original mechanisms of oral aggression.

> The role, which the super-ego undertakes later in life, is at first played by an external power, by parental authority. The influence of the parents dominates the child by granting proof of affection and by threats of punishment, which, to the child, means loss of love, and which also must be feared on their own account. This objective anxiety is the forerunner of the later moral anxiety; so long as the former is dominant one need not speak of super-ego or of conscience. It is only later that the secondary situation arises, which we are far too ready to regard as the normal state of affairs; the external restrictions are introjected, so that the super-ego takes the place of the parental function, and thenceforward observes, guides and threatens the ego in just the same way as the parents acted to the child before. . . . The basis of the process is what we call an identification, that is to say, that one ego becomes like another, one which results in the first ego behaving itself in certain respects in the same way as the second; it imitates it, and as it were takes it into itself. This identification has been not inappropriately compared with the oral cannibalistic incorporation of another person.[7]

When the child is prevented, for whatever reason, from carrying out the aims of the Oedipus complex, imaginatively,

7. Sigmund Freud, *New Introductory Lectures* (New York: Norton, 1933), pp. 89–90.

the Oedipus complex will not be resolved. When this child becomes an adult, he or she will not hear the voice of conscience coming from inside but will continue to hear it from outside; the superego will not be internalized. The greater the degree to which Oedipal goals are accomplished imaginatively, the more the superego will be internalized and listened to unambivalently. Primitive society succeeded in defusing the power in Oedipal feelings; civilized culture realizes in an unconscious manner (a realization that is incorporated into cultural forms) that if we are to grow up, we must be prepared to do imaginatively what the Oedipus complex asks us to do. The quality and the power of conscience depend upon it.

Substitution as a mechanism of sublimation has already been illustrated in this book. In chapter 2, the manner of killing the old on the Island of Vate in the New Hebrides was discussed. Aged people were put to death by burying them alive. The victim was placed in a hole with a live pig tied to each arm. Before the grave was closed, the pigs were released; they were subsequently killed and eaten. Instead of eating the corpse, the people ate the pigs.

Why does such a simple substitution work? It works because the desire to give up eating the corpse precedes the substitution of the pigs; the substitution itself does not cause the sublimation of the desire to eat the corpse. The unconscious wish for sublimation is already in existence to a strong enough degree that the sublimation may become a reality. The substitution of the pigs is the *enabling act;* the corpse is eaten imaginatively when the pigs are eaten actually. The imagination can do its work, but it is not yet strong enough to do it without assistance; it must be aided by some reminder of what is being given up. Without the pigs, the imagination cannot do its symbolic work; they are necessary because the attitude towards eating the corpse is, essentially, ambivalent. There exists both the desire to eat the corpse and the wish to renounce such activity. The substitution of the pigs satisfies both sides of the ambivalence—the corpse is not eaten, but something else is.

We must not think of cannibalism as the basic nonsymbolic act of aggression and of all subsequent, sublimated aggression as symbolic of it. *Cannibalism itself is the result of a symbolic act.* To kill the original objects of aggression—one's parents—is a psychotic act. Yet, cannibals are not psychotic; they are adults in a very primitive state of culture. In the social context, cannibalism is an elementary form of aggression. To exist as a form, however, is to exist in a state that already owes something to sublimation and symbolization. One of the features of a psychotic is that he is incapable of certain symbolic actions—he is compelled to act out certain feelings directly, with no (or minimal) sublimation.

Restriction, the third mechanism of sublimation, occurs in circumstances where specific acts of aggression are restricted to certain members of society and are enjoyed by all the other members in a vicarious way (*vicarious* being another way of saying *imaginative*). The cannibal society of the Kwakiutl is a perfect illustration of this mechanism; all other situations of restriction operate on the same principle of vicarious satisfaction.

The Characteristic Mode of Aggression within Our Own Society

Before I leave this discussion of sublimation and the development of culture, I want to try to answer the question what is the characteristic mode of aggression in our own society? The mode of aggression characteristic of the worst of our society lies in the less sublimated primitive past—those social desires represented by reactionary thinking. Racism, fascism, the restriction of individual liberty, and aggressive war are the forms that this regressive aggression takes.

The liberal has no sympathy with such views. Being free of reactionary impulses, he thinks that he is free of aggressive desires; he looks upon himself as a good person. He does not consciously understand that he has completely adopted the characteristic mode of aggression within the society—the most respectable, accepted mode of aggression. The attitudes of this mode are so internalized that the average liberal person does not see them as aggressive; he sees them as right and proper, as people always have. It is only in a time of crisis, such as the one caused by the failure of American military might to win a quick victory in Southeast Asia (a goal that was originally supported by most liberals), that he vaguely begins to understand that there is a characteristic mode of aggression within the best of the cultures in which he lives. It goes by the name of competition, and capitalism is the economic system that embodies this aggression in the Western world, just as a nonlibertarian state socialism embodies this aggressive mode east of the Elbe.

Competition is itself a wonderfully sublimated mode of action. Like the Kwakiutl, we also "fight with property"; similarly, our fighting with property can quickly degenerate into fighting with weapons. Schumpeter,[8] points out that capitalism represents a great cultural advance over feudalism because it becomes possible for men to prove their manliness without having to go out and kill someone; this is undoubtedly true. Competition replaces warfare as the characteristic mode of aggression. Conservatives pay honor to the last great sublimation and insist that we have now found the ultimate form of human society and should proceed no further. It is clear that competition has replaced warfare, but to contemplate that competition itself could ever be replaced—that, to many, is obviously nonsense.

I do not mean to imply that a change of the capitalist system must, in itself, produce an elimination of competition as a mode of aggression; the Soviet Union has shown that this is not so. It is not capitalism as such that is characteristic of the cultural system but the element of competition. However, in a democratic society that sets itself the goal of bringing about a new era of the sublimation of aggression, capitalism as we know it will not long endure. A culture that sublimates and transforms the aggressive mode of competition is not compatible with an economic system that insists that many people must lose in order that some people can be winners.

8. Joseph Schumpeter, *Capitalism, Socialism and Democracy* (New York: Harper, 1950).

Competition is aggression; it is aggression because it implies that one person can be successful only if others are not. One does not have to kill or enslave others to domineer over them; one can do it in a civilized manner. This is the true meaning of competition: competition means that someone else must lose if I am to win. It means that we cannot all be winners; to be winners, there must be losers. To insist upon the necessity of losers is an aggressive act.

The humane liberal in our society truly does not want to regress into more primitive modes of aggression. He has no desire to enslave anybody or take away liberties or "zap yellow gooks." But he believes in competition. He has his success to enjoy; whether he be a lawyer or a teacher or a businessman, he has become a success by competing with others. He has the constant image of the failure of others, or the smaller success of others, to reassure him in his manliness.

For this reason, he finds it almost impossible to separate himself from the basic cultural attitudes of society. Yes, he says, we should have gotten out of Vietnam; but when one raises the question of how we got there in the first place, one gets a look of consternation because such a question goes to the very heart of the meaning of competition as aggression. He will not consciously see that we killed those people because they rejected our notion that the philosophy of competition should rule the world.

People are reluctant to give up their characteristic way of satisfying their aggressiveness. The prejudiced man will attack you if you tell him he must give up his racism; the authoritarian will do the same if you tell him he must allow individual liberty. The cannibal thought anthropophagy was a necessary human activity; the average good person in our society feels the same about competition. He will insist that people are not motivated to act without the carrot of competition; the Prussian felt the same way about warfare. It satisfies the basic human needs of manliness and ambition, we will be told about competition; head-hunting was as satisfying of these emotions. Finally, the average American will insist that without competition society would not be possible. Hobbes told us the same about authority; hundreds of others told us the same about religious sanctions of morality.

Average people who hold these views do not want others to suffer, but they do want to make sure there is a social pyramid on which they are somewhere near the top. This is highly sublimated aggression and truly civilized, but it is a socially institutionalized form of aggression, and it is capable of still further transformation.

The moral task of our culture is not merely to fulfill the ideals of our society but also to change those ideals to include a new order of sublimation. The real hypocrisy in our culture is the pretense that people in the culture are leading unaggressive lives. This moral transformation will not come about unless we understand the culture under which we now live and its characteristic mode of aggression (genus: aggression; species: competition). As long as capitalism remains the characteristic form of our economic system, the possibilities of such a transformation are indeed slim.

The Cultural Significance of Sublimation

The significance of sublimation is that it makes cultural form possible and makes the development of that form a goal within the capacity of human beings. When sexual, aggressive, and magical energies are sublimated, they continue as sexual, aggressive, and magical manifestations, but in the process of sublimation, energy is made available to the psyche. When these feelings are sublimated into less primitive forms, they lose some of their original pristine nature. Yet, the psyche is like the physical world; energy cannot be destroyed. The psychic energy released when aggressive, sexual, and magical instincts are sublimated can be used to construct new forms.

The development of the superego is one important result of the release of these energies. By superego I do not mean merely moral conscience in a limited sense, although that is a part of the superego. In addition to asking that we love our neighbors as ourselves, the superego also asks that we grow up and become mature. It takes a stand against regressive satisfactions, it encourages us to be human and adult in the fullest sense of the words, and it takes a stand against magic in favor of reality. The cultural superego (institutionalized norms) is also capable of development. The cultural superego of an ancient Roman is not the same as that of someone living in the twentieth century. It is primarily the sublimation of aggressive instincts and the consequent release of energy that makes this development possible. The power in the "idea whose time has come" is a new power released through the sublimation of more primitive, or less civilized, drives.

The superego plays a double role: on the one hand, it is a product of sublimation; on the other, it is an advocate of further sublimation. Its power grows in the giving up of primitive forms; it uses that power to urge further development. Individually, the great gift of sublimation is a free, mature ego. Socially, that great gift is the development of cultural form.

9 The Ambiguity of Development

Although I have postulated cannibalism as the elementary form of institutionalized aggression and a developmental theory of cultural growth from cannibalism, I do not mean to say that all human cultures were, at their beginning, cannibalistic, or that all cultural change in regard to cannibalism moves from a cannibalistic to a noncannibalistic culture, or that all noncannibal cultures are of a higher order of development than all cannibal cultures. The development of cultural-religious forms is not simple; it is ambiguous. One must simplify the evidence first, in order to make a valid theoretical statement about it; but in the process of simplification one loses something, although more is gained than lost. After this simplification has been accomplished and insight has been gained, one is obliged to reintroduce the complexities of the situation so that understanding and theory correspond more closely to reality. In this final chapter, I wish to discuss the data I have found that indicates the path from cannibalism to civilization was much more complicated than any simple theoretical approach can allow for.

Were All Cultures Originally Cannibalistic?

Within the present state of our knowledge, this question cannot be answered. We have no idea about the origin of human society. There is some indication that the very earliest people practiced some form of cannibalism, but the evidence is hardly conclusive. *Sinathropos* (Peking man, recently classified as *Homo erectus*) has been dated by some to have lived one million years ago.

> The bodies had been decapitated after death, buried until they had decomposed, and the heads were then carefully preserved for ritual purposes, doubtless, as in Borneo today, because in them it was supposed that soul-subtance resided having the properties of a vitalizing agent. As the skulls show signs of injuries they may have been those of victims who had been killed and their crania broken open in order to extract the brain for sacramental consumption. If this were so, probably they represent the remains of cannibal feasts.[1]

In certain paleolithic sites, the evidence for cannibalism is a little stronger, but not more than that.

> In the Ngandoery terraces of the Solo River in Eastern Java (which may correspond in time to the Riss-Würm Interglacial in Europe) skulls appear to have been hacked open, possibly at a cannibal feast, and subsequently used as bowls. Thus, in an Upper Paleolithic cave at Placard, Charente drinking cups made from the upper part of the vault of human skulls occurred in the Magdalenian and Soluterean layers. At Krapira near Zagreb in Croatia in a Mousterian deposit on a terrace which also belongs to the Riss-Würm Interglacial, a quantity of human and animal bones occurred in a fragmentary condition, some having been split open to obtain their marrow and charred, suggesting the remains of a cannibal feast.[2]

The rest is silence.

Is All Cultural Movement Away from Cannibalism?

There are many known instances of primitive peoples who were not cannibals and who then proceeded to take up the

1. E. O. James, *Prehistoric Religion* (New York: Barnes and Noble, 1957), p. 18.
2. Ibid., p. 19.

practice, invariably under the influence of neighboring cannibal peoples. Of the peoples of the Sudan, Spence observes:

> The first instances of cannibalism amongst them were invariably stated to have occurred shortly after their conquest by the Azande. But the most striking testimony is afforded by the convincing description one gets in all districts of the way in which one tribe after another from west to east acquired in turn the cannibal habit as they fell under Zande sway. This wave of cannibalism which swept the Southern Bahr el Ghazal spread just so far as the wave of Zande conquest and spent itself in the outlying parts where Zande influence was most recent, till it was finally checked by civilization.[3]

In the Congo, Hinde reports on a rather ironic result of the pacification of the country by Europeans. In pre-Eruopean times, noncannibal people who wandered among surrounding cannibal tribes were killed and eaten, not living to tell the tale. As a result of European influence, travelers were protected, returned to their own tribes, informed them of their new knowledge of the pleasures of eating human flesh, and thus introduced anthropophagy into situations where it had not recently existed.[4]

Boas informs us that the restricted cannibalism practiced by the Kwakiutl was acquired by them from the Hē'iltsuq about sixty years before his work was done; the custom was also acquired by the Tsimshian from the same source no more than seventy years previously. "Therefore there is no doubt that the custom was originally confined to the small territory of the Hē'iltsuq."[5]

Codrington relates a situation of expanding cannibalism in Melanesia. The natives of Florida reported that human flesh was never eaten except at times of sacrifice; the sacrifice of humans itself was introduced in recent times from further

3. Basil Spence, "Cannibalism in the El Ghazal," in *Sudan Notes and Records* 3 no. 4 (December 1920): 302.
4. S. L. Hinde, *The Fall of the Congo Arabs* (London: Methuen, 1897), p. 66.
5. Boas, *Social Organization and Secret Societies of the Kwakiutl Indians*, p. 669.

west. At Saa, anthropophagy was not practiced in previous times, and the elder men had nothing to do with it. The younger men had begun the practice of eating the bodies of enemies slain in battle, having learned this custom from men of the eastern coast who had lived with them and from the Bauro men of San Cristoval whom they had visited.[6]

When Captain Cook visited Tonga, the practice of cannibalism was unknown, but subsequently the Tongans learned it from the Fijians. It never became a universally accepted practice, however. When some tribesmen returned from an expedition, and it became known that they had eaten human flesh, others in the village, especially the women, would avoid them. They would even be subject to abuse: " '*Ta—whe moe ky-tangata!*'—'Keep off! You are eaters of human flesh.' "[7]

What we do not know, since we do not have any historical data, is whether these are cases of reversion to cannibalism or whether they represent the very first time such cultures engaged in cannibal activity. When the Kwakiutl adapted the practice of anthropophagy from the Hē'iltsuq, was this the first time in the history of the Kwakiutl when cannibalism was practiced? Was there a previous time, unrecorded, when cannibalism was given up? And if so, how long did that time last? How many previous abandonments and readoptions of cannibalism had the Kwakiutl gone through before Boas began to make a record of their history?

We do know that in all the cases that are recorded where peoples began to be cannibalistic, that the practice was adopted from another tribe. We also know that there are many situations, especially in Nigeria and New Guinea, where cannibal and noncannibal peoples existed in very close proximity to and contact with each other. In this latter circumstance, it would not be surprising to find any particular tribe moving, culturally, in either direction. I would even venture to say that if one took an area like Nigeria, where a large number of tribes existed, some cannibal, some not, and

6. Codrington, *Melanesians*, pp. 343–344.

7. A. P. Rice, "Cannibalism in Polynesia," in *The American Antiquarian* 32 (1910): 80; Hogg, *Cannibalism and Human Sacrifice*, p. 160, quoting Dr. John Martin.

had been able to make a survey in 1650, 1750, and 1850 to determine which tribes were anthropophagous, that one would have found great variation from one census to the next.

Do All Cannibal Tribes Represent a Lower Cultural Development?

The terms lower or higher, as descriptive terms applied to culture, can easily become entirely too subjective. We do have enough information, however, to conclude that being anthropophagous did not condemn people to the most primitive level of cultural development. If a particular tribe engaged in cannibal activity, it did not follow that the tribe was incapable of cultural development nor that the tribe would compare unfavorably with its noncannibal neighbors either in the complexity or the richness of its culture.

The data being of a subjective nature, I will quote directly from it. "The impression I received from personal intercourse was that the cannibals of the forest were infinitely more sympathetic than the people of the open country, where the trading instinct is inborn. The cannibals are not schemers, and they are not mean. When they steal they generally grab. Though in direct opposition to all natural conjectures, they are among the best types of men, representing the most enlightened and enterprising of the Congo communities."[8]

Bentley writes of another area of the Congo:

> The whole wide country seemed to be given up to cannibalism, from the Mobangi to Stanley Falls, for 600 miles on both sides of the main river, and the Mobangi as well. Cannibalism is a bad habit, but it does not necessarily mark out the natives who observe it as being of a lower type than others who do not. It is a well-known fact that some of the cannibal peoples of Africa are far in advance of many tribes who would shudder at the very idea. The natives of Manyanga and the Lukunga district of the cataract region were far

8. Herbert Ward, *A Voice from the Congo* (London: Heinemann, 1910), p. 276.

more degraded, and no less cruel and wicked, than the wild cannibals of the Upper Congo; but they would scorn the idea of eating human flesh as much as we would.[9]

The most important comparison of cannibal and noncannibal peoples comes from the appendix of an article by Basil Spence, written by the editor of the periodical, who is quoting Dr. Junker about the Mangbattu.

> In other respects also and especially in their higher artistic faculty the Mangbattu show a marked superiority over any other Negro peoples; yet they otherwise stand at the lowest level of culture—at least if cannibalism is decisive on that point. This practice is more widespread amongst them even than amongst the Niam-Niams. But it cannot serve as a final test in estimating the relative position of uncultured races, as determined by their general capacity and mental qualities. Why some of these more highly gifted races should be addicted to anthropophagy remains an unsolved riddle, but the fact is beyond dispute. The inhabitants of the equatorial region within the Congo basin are also more or less cannibals; yet they take a high position amongst the riverain populations in respect of their intellectual faculties. The same impression was produced on me in comparing the various races in the regions comprised within the sphere of my explorations. Thus the Bari of the Bohr el Jebel can hardly be compared from the intellectual standpoint either with the Zandehs or the Mangbattus; yet like all the Negroes dwelling in the eastern and northern provinces they hold human flesh in abomination. The practice earned for the Zandehs the nickname of Niam-Niam just as their easternmost tribes, the Idio and Bomba, are known as Mukuraka, both terms having the same meaning of "man-eater."[10]

Cannibalism, or more accurately, the social expression of aggression, is only one test of a culture. The relative primitiveness of the expression of aggression is only one factor in the total cultural form; it is not the sole determinant. The purpose of this book has been to demonstrate the extreme importance that the expression of aggression plays in the

9. Bentley, *Pioneering on the Congo,* p. 210.
10. Spence, "Cannibalism in El Ghazal," pp. 302–303.

formation and development of culture; nowhere is it claimed that this is the only factor or even, necessarily, the most important one. One cannot judge the culture of fifth-century Athens on the basis of the destruction of the island of Melos and the killing of every male adult therein, but one cannot ignore this incident and still understand the culture of this great people. Cannibals can have a higher culture than noncannibal peoples because the expression of aggression is only one factor that determines the cultural status. Yet, I do not want to minimize the primitiveness of the cannibal act. In such a circumstance, we must say that such a culture is most primitive in the way it expresses and satisfies aggression, but that in other areas of culture it has advanced beyond its neighbors.

The same is true of human beings in their personal lives. An adult in our society relates to many different things: job, spouse, children, other people, and the culture as a whole. One is usually surprised, but not shocked, on discovering a great disparity in the way someone acts in these various areas; a person may easily be very competent in some things, relatively incompetent in others, and a failure in still others. Cultural development is certainly no less complex than individual development.

Some Other Considerations of Cannibal Life

Of the southern Massim, who are devout cannibals, Seligmann writes: "In the vast majority of cases family life seems to be calm and happy in spite of the sudden gusts of uncontrollable passion to which many Papuo-Melanesians seem liable at times. . . . Both sexes make affectionate and indeed over-indulgent parents, while the children brought up under these conditions make as a rule excellent sons, daughters and even relations-in-law, and no old man or old woman . . . is neglected by his or her children or grandchildren. . . ." The cannibal life, however, is a dangerous one. "A man's wife one day cooked some food for their pig, and, putting it on some leaves, placed it outside the house for the pig to eat. Her husband's dog came up and, chasing the pig away, began to eat the food. The woman then took up a small stone and threw it at the dog, with the intention of driving it away. Her husband in a frenzy of passion immediately jumped up from the place where he had been sitting, and seizing a pointed stick drove it with such fatal effect into his wife's body, that she expired on the spot."[11] Seligmann does not contend that this kind of incident is necessarily widespread in the culture, but it is one example of "sudden gusts of uncontrollable passion." In culture, cannibalism is only one factor; in aggression, it is crucial.

Civilized people are not the only ones who find something fearful in cannibalism; it is comforting to learn that cannibals themselves can be afraid of cannibalism. This fear is useful in the development of culture. It would not be an exaggeration to say that if there was nothing to fear in cannibalism it would never have been given up. It is also interesting to learn that, as with our version of cannibalism—racism—it does not come naturally to children and has to be taught.

In Melanesia, the man who cut up the body wore something over his mouth and nose to keep the spirit of the dead man from entering into him. While the body was being eaten, the doors of the house were shut; afterwards, the people all shouted, blew horns, and shook spears to drive away the ghosts of the men eaten. On the Duke of York Island, many of the people were too fearful to look at the body while it was being cooked. Many, *especially girls and boys,* refused to eat it out of fear.[12]

When the natural desire to give up cannibalism is strengthened by outside force, the transition can occur with great swiftness. At Orokolo in New Guinea, after the conquest of the country by Europeans, the neighboring cannibal peoples of Namau found themselves subject to great derision because of their fondness for human flesh. The people of

11. Seligmann, *Melanesians of British New Guinea,* pp. 566, 566n.
12. Reverend G. Brown, *Melanesians and Polynesians* (London: Macmillan & Co., 1910), pp. 145–146.

Orokolo, who were not cannibals at the time of the conquest, refused to allow the Namau to enter the precincts of their villages. The Namau deeply resented these insults; in the old days they would have replied simply by driving the Orokolo people out of their own villages. Under the circumstances of European control, this was impossible. Their only recourse was to give up anthropophagy, whereupon they were accepted into Orokolo society. This action by the Namau village of Maipua excited the jealousy of another Namau village, called Kaimare, and they also gave up eating human flesh.[13]

There is one documented case of a regression to cannibal behavior, not by a whole culture, but within the confines of a secret society: the Mau Mau society in Kenya. The regression was caused by the extreme stress of revolt against white domination and occurred during an attempt to reassert the prominence of tribal society. The Mau Mau engaged in a complicated ritual of oath-taking that came to include cannibal elements. The fourth oath, taken before becoming a captain in the Mau Mau army, required the presence of a dead body. At the oath-taking ceremony, the fingers of the dead man were bent seven times and his eyes pricked seven times. A major, or a treasurer, taking the fifth oath, was required to bite the brain of a dead African seven times. A brigadier took the sixth oath; he was required to eat seven pieces from the brain of a European man. A general took the seventh oath, which required him also to eat, besides the brain, the wrist bones of a European man. The last oath, which bound a member never to disclose the whereabouts of weapons and ammunition, required the presence of a dead child and a dead man. The heart of the child was cut out and pricked seven times; the brain and blood of the dead man were mixed with the blood of the oath-takers, and the mixture was drunk.[14]

In times of great stress, a culture may revert to more primitive forms of expressing aggression. Such regression is pathological—the sign of a sick society. True cannibals are

13. Murray, *Papua, or British New Guinea*, pp. 172–173.
14. Ione Leigh, *In the Shadow of the Mau Mau* (London: W. H. Allen, 1954), p. 40.

not living in a sick society; their cultural development is merely very primitive. To be a cannibal because your mother and father were cannibals is one thing; to become a cannibal when your mother and father were not is an entirely different thing. The experience of Nazi Germany is one of a society in a state of psychotic breakdown. The deliberate destruction of millions of people, the lamp shades of human skin, the pulling of gold out of the teeth of the dead—all this is not true cannibalism, but it is as close to it as any "civilized" society has come in an institutionalized form.

The culture of Germany was clearly under a tremendous strain before the Nazis took power; the strain was so great that the civilizing forces in the society disintegrated. The expression of aggression is a crucial aspect of the cultural system, and when that system disintegrates, it is inevitable that the satisfaction of aggressive needs sink to a more primitive level. The current wave of more primitive violence in our own society is a sign of great cultural stress, which is inducing some members of the culture to regress to more primitive ways of expressing aggressive drives.

Cannibalism and the Elementary Forms of Cultural Life

One can imagine human beings in a state without language or without religion of any kind, which is not to say that humans ever existed without either. No primitive culture has been discovered that did not have both. The purpose of this exercise is not to test a postulate about historical reality. Instead, if we can imagine what it would be like to be conscious without language or religion, we can gain insight into the functions language and religion serve for human beings. In other words, if we can grasp some idea of what life would be like without these forms, we can postulate what human emotions and institutions language and religion make possible. The same exercise may be conducted about culture itself. Let us try to imagine human beings without culture, or with a minimal amount of culture. If we can do this with any success, we may begin to see what culture actually does for human life.

Life without culture may involve groups of adults, either one male and one female, or other combinations, traveling with pre-pubescent children. When the child becomes pubescent, its sexual drives cannot be satisfied within the family group; it therefore leaves and sets about finding a mate in the woods in order to begin its own family. Such is the life of the orangutang. It is a life without culture, although certain cultural elements, such as language and weapons, may exist.

Cultural beginnings would take place if the pubescent children did not leave the nuclear family but stayed with it even after marriage. We can imagine small family bands moving through the forest in search of game to eat. Such groups would consist of adults, pre-pubescent children, and the married children of the adults. These latter would be in the circumstance of raising their own children within the traveling family band. It is a picture presented to us, romantically glossed over, of the situation of the patriarchs in the Old Testament: Jacob with his two wives and two concubines, their twelve children, the spouses of these children, and the grandchildren of Jacob all traveling together.

In more primitive circumstances than those in the story of Jacob, there would be no settled people living in villages or cities. All the world would consist of these traveling bands of families. Marriage would take place between the various bands; either the male or the female would stay with its family; marriage could be arranged between family groups, or else kidnaping might be used in obtaining a spouse.

This hypothetical situation of the family horde represents an intolerable human burden compared with even the most primitive culture that has been discovered. In such horde circumstances, everyone is related to everyone else. No one can commit any act of aggression without injuring the family; no one can commit an act of sexual aberration without being very destructive to family solidarity. There would be no clan, no tribe, no organized and developing religious ritual, no initiation ceremonies for pubescent children, no men's or women's clubs, no kinship system that relieves the burden of relating only to father and mother, no organized method of warfare that directs aggression outward, and no satisfaction of sexual feelings except in a family context. It is no wonder that in imagining such a predicament Freud came up with a nightmare: the father would keep all the women to himself and the brothers would be forced to rise up and kill him in order to have any sexual satisfaction.

The possibilities of sexual, aggressive, and magical sublimation in the circumstance of the family horde are minimal. The true function of culture is to provide the possibilities of these sublimations. This is accomplished by creating a world larger than the family, so that these instincts do not have to be dealt with strictly in a family context. All cultural situations, no matter how primitive, provide rules concerning sexual, aggressive and magical behavior. Sexual feelings are directed away from the family, aggressive instincts are released away from the clan or tribe, and magical attitudes are given room to expand into the areas of art and religion. The formation and functioning of conscience is also released from the confines of the family; there is an appeal over the heads of the parents to the culture as a whole in moral questions. In fact, the culture as a whole takes the place of the parents in dictating the moral imperatives.

What the cultural situation does is to make it possible to leave the family without actually going away. In the imagined circumstance of the family horde, to free oneself of the burdens of living within the family, one was forced to go away forever; the choice was to stay home in a situation of great stress or to leave. Culture provides a solution to this dilemma. One can preserve the continuity of family life within a situation that provides room for sublimation and development; one is not forced to go away in order to leave. The nature of form lies in its capacity to hold together contradictory or ambivalent things. The two human desires to preserve family attachments and to live one's own life are in opposition to each other; within cultural form, both these desires are satisfied.

Sexuality, aggression, magic, and morality—these are the great parameters of human culture. Any successful search for the elementary forms of cultural life must pay particular attention to these fundamental human instinctual needs. Cannibalism is the fundamental form of institutionalized aggression—it is impossible to comprehend the true nature of human culture without understanding its role in human history.

INDEX

Abraham, Karl, 81
Affectionate cannibalism, 22–34
Aggression
- psychological origin of, 64–82
- religion and, 99–110
- uses of, 83–98

Aggressive cannibalism, 1–21
Albania, 31
Amazon, 18–19, 26
Anal sadism, 69
Angas, 23
Art, 123–124
Australia, 2, 25, 26
Azande, 134
Aztec Indians, 1–2, 48, 55, 60–61

Bacchae (Euripides), xx
Bangalas, 53
Bantoc, 44
Basden, G. T., 58–59
Bauro, 135
Bavaria, 31
Bear Dancers, 13
Benin, Nigeria, 56
Bentley, W. Holman, 136–137
Beyond the Pleasure Principle (Freud), 85–86
Binandele, 16
Boas, Franz, 134
Burma, 43
Burton, R. V., 90

Capitalism, xvi, 110, 128–130
Cassirer, Ernst, 50
Chawai, 39
Child, Irvin S., 72, 88, 93
Child Training and Personality (Whiting and Child), 88
Child-rearing practices, 83–95
Christianity, xvi, 60–63, 105
Circumcision, 97–98
Civilization and Its Discontents (Freud), 66–67
Codrington, R. H., 134
Competition, 128–130
Congo, 2, 53, 102–103, 134, 136–137
Cross-sex identity, 87
Crucifixion, 49
Cultural relativism, 82

Dependence, 83–98
Doll's House, A (Ibsen), 84

Dostoevski, Fëdor, xx
Durkheim, Émile, 99, 108

Edo, 56
Ego, 69–70
Essay on Man, An (Cassirer), 50
Euripides, xx

Fairy tales, xx
Fascism, xvii, 105, 127
Fears, 100, 101, 139
Female infanticide, xvi, 105
Feudalism, 128
Fiji, 2, 10, 54–55, 57, 135
Fool Dancers, 13
Frazer, James G., 57, 121
Freud, Sigmund, 14, 32, 33, 50–51, 61, 69, 70, 71, 77–79, 85–86, 108–109, 119, 124, 143
Funeral ritual, 3, 23, 26, 29, 31–33, 53–54

Genital aggression, 69
Gopi ceremony, 18
Greece, ancient, 62
Guilt, 72

Hā'mats'a, 12–15, 24, 113
Hartland, Edwin Sidney, 30
Head-hunting, 35–47, 105
Hē'iltsuq Indians, 134, 135
Hinde, S. L., 134
Hindus, 32
Hobbes, Thomas, 130
Howitt, A. W., 26
Huron Indians, 10

Ibsen, Henrik, 84
Ida, 43
Imperialism, 106, 110
Imunu, 9
Incest, 74
Independence, 83–98
Initiation ceremonies, 90–91, 96, 97–98
Instinctual drive, 64–82, 85–86
Iroquois Indians, 9, 75
Islam, xvi, 105
Israel, ancient, 62
Iwa, Melanesia, 29
Iwi, New Guinea, 26

Jews, 105
Jibaro Indians, 35–37, 42–44

Kagaro, 39
Kant, Immanuel, xv
Karsten, Rafael, 36, 42, 43
Kawpi purai, 103
Kenya, 140
Kluckhohn, R., 72
Kuekutsa societies, 13
Kwakiutl Indians, 12–15, 24, 37–38, 111–117, 127, 134
Kwoma, 89

Leningrad, siege of, 1
Libido, 77–79, 108–109
Leopard society, 10, 23
Leper's Island, 8
Love, 118–119

Mabuiag, 8
Magic, 101, 121–123
Malinowski, Bronislaw, 119
Mana, 8, 108
Mangbattu, 137
Manliness, 7–8, 37, 44–46
Maoris, 9, 17–18, 57
Masochism, 68
Massim, 138–139

Mau Mau society, 140
Melanesia, 5–6, 29, 56–57, 104, 134, 139
Melos, island of, 138
Molot, 6
Murdock, George, 2, 60, 92

Nagir, 8
Namau, New Guinea, 139–140
Navaho Indians, 72
Nazis, 141
New Guinea, 2, 3–4, 16, 18, 20, 26, 45, 102, 135, 139–140
New Hebrides, 29, 126
Nigeria, 2, 23, 37, 44, 45, 53, 56, 57, 135

Oedipus complex, 64, 69–72, 124–126
Old people, 19, 23, 29, 126
Oral aggression, 69, 70, 72–73, 80
Oral incorporation, 9, 28
Orang Sakei, 33
Orokaiva, New Guinea, 6, 16
Orokolo, New Guinea, 139–140
Our Primitive Contemporaries (Murdock), 2

Papua, New Guinea, 30, 45
Pawnee Indians, 49, 57
Philippine Islands, 44
Philosophy of Symbolic Forms, The (Cassirer), 50
Polynesia, 4
Potlatch, 111–112, 115–116
Profane, definition of, 99–102
Pulu, 7–8
Purari Delta, New Guinea, 18
Pygmies, xviii

Racism, 106, 110, 127, 139
Radin, Paul, 53
Relatives, 22–33
Religion, aggression and, 99–110
Revenge, 5–7, 36–37
Ritual activities, 14–20

Saa, 135
Sacred, definition of, 100–102
Sacrifice, 48–63, 68, 95–98, 108, 113–114, 134
Sadism, 9–11, 37, 68
San Cristoval, Solomon Islands, 135
Sarawak, Borneo, 44, 45–46
Schumpeter, Joseph, 128
Science, 123–124
Self-destruction, 67–68
Seligmann, C. G., 5–6, 104, 138, 139
Sexual activity, 100–101, 108–109, 117–121
Shakespeare, William, 123
Shame, 72
Sierra Leone, 10
Sinathropos, 133
Sindh, India, 32
Slater, Philip, 84, 94
Slavery, xvi, 110
Social Darwinism, xvii
Solomon Islands, 9, 37
Spence, Basil, 134, 137
Spock, Benjamin, 95
Stephens, William, 92
Sublimation, 28–31, 40, 111–131
Sudan, 134
Sumatra, 33
Superego, 69–70, 124–126, 130–131

Taboos, 14–16, 108
Tangara, 26
Tariána Indians, 26
Tempest, The (Shakespeare), 123
Thanatos, 67
Togo, New Guinea, 26
Tonga, 135
Torres Straits, 7–8
Torture, 5–6, 10–11
Totem and Taboo (Freud), 14
Trobrianders, 119
Tsimshian Indians, 134
Tucános, 26
Tugarians, 3–4
Turrbal tribes, 25

Vate, island of, 29, 126
Vikings, 3

Wales, 32
Warfare, 3–4, 5–6, 36, 110
Whiting, Beatrice, 87
Whiting, John, 72, 87, 88, 93
Williams, F. E., 16, 18, 20
World Ethnographic Sample (Murdock), 92
Women, 19, 106, 110

Yoruba, 56, 58–59
Yungur, 39–40

Zuñi Indians, xviii

74 75 76 77 78 79 80 12 11 10 9 8 7 6 5 4 3 2 1